The GRANNIES' Book

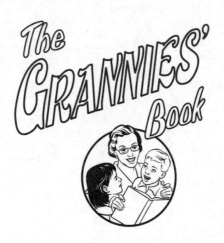

Dear Elaine,
Welcome to the best
Club in the world.
Love
Caroline.
X

The GRANNIES' Book

FOR THE GRANNY WHO'S

Best AT Everything

ALISON MALONEY

Michael O'Mara Books Limited

First published in Great Britain in 2008 by
Michael O'Mara Books Limited
9 Lion Yard, Tremadoc Road
London SW4 7NQ

A CIP catalogue record for this book is available
from the British Library

Papers used by Michael O'Mara Books Limited are
natural, recyclable products made from wood grown in
sustainable forests. The manufacturing processes conform
to the environmental regulations of the country of origin.

ISBN 978-1-84317-251-2

3 5 7 9 10 8 6 4 2

www.mombooks.com

Cover image and illustrations on pages 9, 10, 11, 12, 14, 16, 17, 19, 23,
27, 30, 35, 42, 46, 49, 54, 60, 63, 64, 66, 68, 70–1, 72–3, 74–5, 76, 83,
85, 88, 90, 93, 95, 99–100, 101, 103, 108, 111, 115, 119, 124, 127, 131,
133, 136, 139, 142, 146, 150 and 157 © David Woodroffe 2008

Cover design by Angie Allison
from an original design by www.blacksheep-uk.com

Designed and typeset by Martin Bristow

Printed and bound in Great Britain by Clays Ltd, St Ives plc

To Mum, Dad, Kath and Gerry – the best grandparents my children could have

Contents

CONTENTS

Introduction

So, after raising your own children and sitting back for a few years while they make their own way in the world, you receive the delightful news that you're going to become a granny. Suddenly you're surrounded by nappies and screaming babies, and before you know it the house is full of kids and toys again.

Of course, you can take it all in your stride. Having done it all before with your own family you can quickly switch back in to superwoman mode, return to your multi-tasking best, and get on with it.

The granny who's best at everything thinks nothing of rushing home from work to babysit her adorable grandchildren while their stressed mother has a well-earned night out. She's always on the end of the phone when advice is needed and is there in a flash when a family crisis occurs.

She can tell you how to get blackcurrant stains out of baby's best white T-shirt and always knows the best way to get the kids to sleep. Who else can a worried mum turn to when she is juggling work and children, and needs a helping hand?

For some grannies, though, much may have changed since their youth, so this quick refresher course may be just the thing to pick up a few new childcare tips, find out the best babysitting activities and learn how to deal with the other granny in your grandchild's life.

But never forget that to your grandchildren you will always be the best at everything.

So Now You're a Granny!

You'll never forget that magical moment when you first find out you're going to become a granny. As soon as the joyful news has sunk in, your life changes immediately. Bursting with excitement, before you know it you've started making plans, buying baby clothes and dishing out advice . . .

But whoa – stop right there. Whose baby is this?

The hardest thing for a granny to do is to remember to take a step back and wait to be asked for any help. Although a little gentle guidance may be needed occasionally, it's never wise to undermine the confidence of a new mum or dad by wading in and being overly critical. Most new mums will appreciate well-meaning words of wisdom offered by a parent or mother-in-law, but only up to a point.

The golden rule is *listen to yourself*. If you realize you're starting every sentence with 'You should be . . . ' or 'Why are you . . .' then you're heading for a showdown!

'A mother becomes a true grandmother the day she stops noticing the terrible things her children do because she is so enchanted with the wonderful things her grandchildren do.'

LOIS WYSE

The Times They Have A-changed

*(or Things You Shouldn't Say to the Parents
of Your Grandchild)*

Isn't it time she was out of nappies?

This is a classic mistake most grannies seem unable to avoid, but one that is guaranteed to annoy. Expert advice now leans towards later potty training, and as long as the child is not nearing school age the decision should be left to mum. After all, she's the one who has to deal with the 'accidents'!

Make sure he's well wrapped up.

Sound advice when venturing outside in January, but not necessarily if he is being put to bed in a centrally heated house. Overheating a baby can contribute to Sudden Infant Death Syndrome (SIDS) or cot death. The temperature of the nursery should be between 16°C and 20°C and wrapping a baby tightly in blankets is dangerous.

She shouldn't have a dummy at her age.

OK, so a dummy wedged firmly in the mouth of a five-year-old is not a good look, but it won't actually do any harm. In young babies, research has shown that a dummy at bedtime can help to prevent cot death.

Shouldn't he be lying on his front?

For many grannies, this is a tough one. When your children were young the advice was to lie babies on their stomachs but, in the early 1990s, the 'Back to Sleep' campaign changed things. It was discovered that babies sleeping on their backs were much less likely to die from cot death, and since the change in advice, the number of cot-death victims has fallen by 70 per cent – that's twelve babies a week.

Isn't it time she was on solids?

Weaning used to start at four months, but World Health Organization guidelines now state that it shouldn't begin until the child is six months old. Experts believe that children are healthier if their sole source of nutrition for the first six months is breast milk, although bottled milk is the next best thing.

You can't leave him crying in the cot . . .

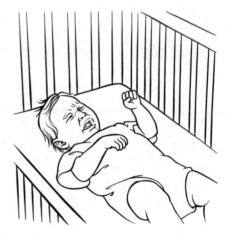

Difficult as it is to hear your beloved grandchild bawling at bedtime, many modern parents use the 'controlled crying' technique for wakeful children over six months. It takes a lot of willpower, but it really does work. Unless the child is genuinely frightened or hysterical, they should be left to cry slightly longer each time, starting at around five minutes (see *Toddler Taming* by Dr Christopher Green for full details). If you go in after that time, stroking and patting is better than lifting and cuddling. All that difficult work will be quickly undone if Granny runs in and gives baby a hug every time she whimpers!

Shouldn't he be in bed by now?

Not everybody believes a rigid routine at bedtime is necessary. While many parents insist on tucking in their little darlings by 7 p.m., it is perfectly acceptable for others to put them to bed whenever they feel the time is right. In fact, for working parents, quality time with their children in the evenings is more important than an inflexible routine.

You won't be going back to work, I hope?

Depending on your age, you may well have raised your children when the majority of mothers stayed at home. Things are very different today. Some women prefer to go back to work, while others opt to become a full-time mum, but the harsh reality of modern life is that, with mortgage payments dependent on two sets of wages, many mothers work because they have to.

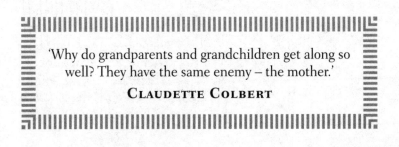

'Why do grandparents and grandchildren get along so well? They have the same enemy – the mother.'
CLAUDETTE COLBERT

What Are Grandmothers Made Of?

Grandparents today are younger, healthier and more active than ever before, and the blue rinse brigade is officially a thing of the past. According to a 2007 survey conducted for *Saga* magazine for the Future Foundation, the average person in the UK becomes a grandparent at the age of forty-nine and spends thirty-five years in this blissful stage of their lives.

The survey also identified five distinct types of grandparents. Which one are you?

Racy role models – younger grandparents who are still employed and active, they enjoy spending time with their grandchildren just for fun and get involved in most activities. They have a diverse social life, enjoying the occasional tipple, flirt and dance, and account for 5 million people, or 37 per cent, of grandparents in the UK.

Hearts of gold – kind and friendly, these grandparents devote a huge amount of time to their grandchildren. They are very sociable with their immediate friends and family, but are not likely to seek out new friends and experiences. There are 0.75 million in the UK, which equates to 6.3 per cent of grandparents.

Adventure seekers – the more affluent grandparent, predominantly female, leading a hectic and full life. The adventure seeker is constantly travelling, in search of fun and new experiences, but she also does a lot for charity and finds time to be with her grandchildren. She is smart and stylish, and concerned with her appearance. There are 2.5 million adventure seekers, making up 19.5 per cent of grandparents in the UK.

Traditionalists – often older grandparents, these are mostly women with a limited range of pastimes. They may have more grandchildren than most, but they are less active and therefore contribute little to the childcare. There are 4 million in the UK, i.e. 31.2 per cent of grandparents.

Quiet reminiscers – this is the smallest group, which mainly comprises men. They are not active and don't choose to spend much time with their grandchildren. They are also less likely to socialize or have hobbies than the other groups. They account for around 0.75 million or 6 per cent of grandparents in the UK.

FASCINATING FACTS AND FIGURES

✳ More than one in five, or 13.3 million, people (22 per cent) in the UK are grandparents. By 2020, it is predicted the number will rise to 16.6 million, which is equivalent to one in four people in the UK or one in three adults over the age of 16.

✳ There are around 56 million grandparents in the United States, of which 5.7 million have their grandchildren living with them.

✳ One in two grandparents have a living parent.

✳ Nearly two-thirds of people aged fifty and over are grandparents.

✳ On average, people spend at least one year where they have a child living at home and are also a grandparent.

✳ The most common age when people become grandparents is just forty-nine years.

✳ By the age of fifty-four, one in every two people is a grandparent.

✳ One in five children under sixteen years old in the UK is looked after in the daytime by grandparents.

✳ More than a third of grandparents spend the equivalent of three days a week caring for their grandchildren.

✳ In the US, 28 per cent of pre-school children with employed mothers are cared for by their grandparents while their mother works.

✳ 1.4 million US grandparents are both working and looking after the basic needs of their grandchildren.

✳ The average UK grandparent has 4.07 grandchildren.

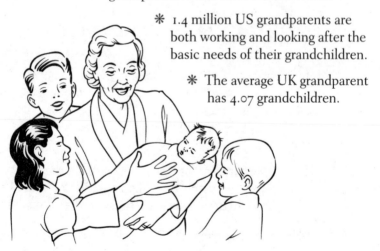

Child-friendly House

It's been a while since you had your own children, and while a quick glance round your house might tell you it's a perfectly safe environment, your son or daughter is guaranteed to disagree. Small children seem to home in on any dangers around them, especially at that crawling, curious stage when they want to investigate the contents of every cupboard and pull everything they can reach down to their level.

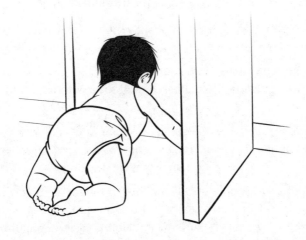

Here are some guidelines to help make your house safer for visiting grandchildren.

✳ Medicines, cleaning fluids and vitamin tablets MUST be locked away in a cupboard that is completely out of children's reach. It takes a split second for a toddler to find a bottle of medicine or bleach, and the consequences could be horrendous.

✳ When using the cooker, put pans on the rear hobs, with the handles turned back. Make sure your kettle is at the back of your work surface and out of grasping distance.

✳ Turn off washing machines, dishwashers and cookers at the mains when not in use.

✳ Put child locks on kitchen cupboards, especially those containing glass or ceramics.

✳ Never keep glasses on a tray on top of a dresser. A toddler can easily reach up and pull it down on top of himself. Move all accessible ornaments to a higher shelf.

✳ Never leave an iron on near a child, even if you are just popping out for a second to hang up a newly ironed garment.

✳ As soon as the child starts to crawl, stair gates, or some means of blocking the stairs, are a must.

✳ Make sure that young children can't open your front door. A bright three-year-old can use a key or find a chair to stand on to undo the latch, and be off down the road before you realize it.

✳ Windows should only be opened at the top, and not wide enough for a child to crawl out. Lock the larger windows and make sure that open windows are not accessible by climbing on beds, sofas etc.

'A house needs a grandma in it.'
LOUISA MAY ALCOTT

BABYSITTING HAZARDS

✳ As the only adult left in the house, you are expected to play endless games of snap.

✳ Babies are happy to play peekaboo for hours!

✳ The minute the parents leave the house, the children will swear that mum said they could stay up late/eat chocolate/watch a DVD.

✳ When you've finally got the kids to bed, there will be nothing you want to watch on TV and you'll wish they were still up.

✳ 'I promise we'll be back by midnight' means you'll be lucky to see the parents before 2 a.m.

✳ You will spend half the night reading 'just one more' bedtime story.

THE LITTLE WHITE LIES
(AND WHAT REALLY HAPPENED)

✴ 'They ate up all their dinner . . .
(plus three cakes, two chocolate bars and a fizzy drink).'

✴ 'They were as good as gold . . .
(until I told them to go to bed).'

✴ 'There were no tantrums at all . . .
(mainly because I let them have their own way all night).'

✴ 'They went to bed at 7.30 on the dot . . .
(give or take an hour or two).'

✴ 'They didn't watch any television . . .
(just played computer games for three hours).'

✴ 'The baby settled beautifully . . .
(after three bottles of milk and two hours of screaming).'

✴ 'I don't mind you being late . . .
(but I was ready for my bed three hours ago).'

✴ 'I had a great evening – ask me any time . . .
(just give me a month or so to recover first).'

'If your baby is "beautiful and perfect, never cries
or fusses, sleeps on schedule and burps on demand,
an angel all the time," you're the grandma.'
TERESA BLOOMINGDALE

GUIDE TO SLEEPOVERS

'Can you have the kids for the weekend?' There comes a time in every grandma's life when they hear these dreaded words and wonder if they are up to the task. Be flattered. No parent would leave their children behind unless they were quite sure they were in safe hands.

There are a few golden rules to stick to when the babysitting session turns into a weekend sleepover.

✳ If your house isn't already stocked with toys,
tell them to bring their own.

✳ If they have special bedtime toys, make sure
they come too. Bedtime without their favourite teddy
is not much fun!

✳ Buy a small gift, such as pens and paper,
paints or crafts, as a distraction for the moment
that the parents say goodbye.

✳ Don't tell very young children that 'Mummy and Daddy are going away.' Instead say 'You're going to come and stay with me so that we can have lots of fun.'

✳ Turn the weekend into an adventure. Think of one or two activities in advance and tell them what they are, so they will look forward to it.

✳ Phone calls to and from parents should be limited to an emergency-only basis. Don't ring Mum to find out where little Molly's toothbrush is or to tell her Molly is refusing to go to bed, and advise Mum and Dad not to call as well. Children are quite capable of forgetting their parents for a few hours and there's nothing like a call from Mummy to remind them that their parents are away, which can lead to tears before bedtime. Out of sight is out of mind for most young kids.

✳ Stick to the parental rules. They might be on your territory now, but their parents won't thank you if the children come home spoiled rotten and refusing to go to bed because 'Granny let us stay up late.'

✳ Don't feed the kids forbidden foods. You may not agree that the children should be denied lemonade and chewy sweets, but it is not your decision to make. Give them treats, by all means, but nothing that would annoy their parents.

✳ Unless you already know them inside out, get parents to write a list of likes and dislikes, so that you're aware of any foods they simply won't eat.

✳ Don't worry if the angelic child you have looked after all weekend turns into a monster when Mum and Dad return. This is a natural reaction and is designed to punish parents for their absence.

HOUSEHOLD ESSENTIALS

If you're looking after your grandchildren at your home, there are a few things you should keep in the house at all times.

First-aid box checklist

* plasters (for young children, the ones with pictures on often help to distract them when they're hurt).

* infant paracetemol syrup (such as Calpol)

* antiseptic cream, spray or wipes (some sprays have anaesthetic qualities to dull the pain – magic!)

* sting-relief pen

* tweezers (for splinters etc.)

* menthol relief (such as Karvol, for blocked noses)

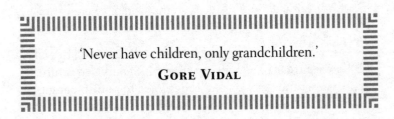

'Never have children, only grandchildren.'
GORE VIDAL

Useful foodstuffs to keep in stock

* Marmite
* tins of tuna
* jam
* milk
* yogurt
* fish fingers
* frozen peas
* eggs
* pasta
* frozen mince (shepherd's pie and spaghetti bolognese are favourites for most kids)
* hot chocolate/cocoa (for late-night milky drinks)

* * *

Grandchildren essentials checklist

For the younger baby:

* changing mat
* nappies
* baby wipes
* barrier cream
* nappy sacks or plastic bags

* bottles

* powdered milk (if bottle-fed)

* sun hat and a winter hat

* spare clothing

For the older baby, add:

* baby bowls

* spoons

* drinking cups

* bibs

* baby food (even if you purée your own food, there are times when a jar or tin is much more convenient)

For all ages:

* toys

* games

* books

* spare clothing (buy cheap T-shirts and trousers at the charity shop and store in a drawer for emergencies; keep hand-me-down wellies for the next grandchild etc.)

* sun hats

* sun cream

Grandma's Kitchen Capers

One of the joys of having grandchildren around is teaching them how to cook. Mums of very young children are often too busy feeding the family to show them how the food is prepared, but grannies have had years of practice, and passing on your skills can be lots of fun.

Try to choose dishes that the kids will enjoy eating as well as cooking, and get them involved in making meals that they don't have at home.

Baking cakes and muffins is ideal, as it means that they can take home the result of their hard work at the end of the day, and share their goodies with mum and dad too.

Working in the kitchen also teaches children what is good for them and what is bad. They may want to bake nothing but chocolate cakes, so try to steer them towards healthier alternatives.

NB. Always remember that safety is very important and young children should be kept away from hot pans, kettles and ovens. It is also wise not to let the children 'lick the bowl' if raw eggs have been used. Experts still advise against eating raw eggs and many parents would not allow their children to lick the spoon or bowl with cake mixture on it.

Here are a few ideas for some great things to make with the grandchildren.

TRADITIONAL LEMONADE

When kids think of lemonade, they usually imagine the clear, fizzy variety in bottles, so this home-made version might take some getting used to. Remember to warn them it will be cloudy and still. A lovely refreshing summer drink with no preservatives or artificial colours in sight, it does, however, contain a lot of sugar, unless you choose the low-sugar alternative shown below.

You will need:
6 lemons • 6 cups of water
1 cup sugar • sprig of fresh mint (optional)

Method:

1. Using a potato peeler, peel the rind from two lemons and squeeze the juice from all six lemons.

2. Place the rind in a bowl, cover with the sugar and pour over one cup of boiling water, then stir to make sure the sugar is properly dissolved. Allow to cool.

3. Strain this syrup into a serving jug, and stir in the juice and the remaining cold water.

4. Add mint, if required, and serve chilled. Makes eight servings.

Make a special pink lemonade by adding a little cranberry juice. For a low-sugar alternative, skip the sugar syrup stage and substitute with 2 cups of white grape juice.

CHICKEN NUGGETS

SERVES FOUR

Most kids adore chicken nuggets, but the shop-bought varieties aren't the most nutritious. These quick-and-easy nuggets will win you the kids' approval, and you (and the children's parents) can rest assured that you know exactly what's in them.

You will need:
500 g (1 lb) boneless chicken breasts
100 g (3.5 oz) fresh breadcrumbs
pinch of salt (optional)
1 egg
5 tbsp of sunflower or rapeseed oil

Method:

1. Cut the chicken breasts into chunks of about 5 cm (2 inches) squared.

2. In a large bowl or shallow dish, mix the breadcrumbs and salt (if used).

3. Beat the egg in a bowl.

4. Dip each chicken piece into the egg, then in the breadcrumbs, turning until they are well coated.

5. Place the chicken pieces in breadcrumbs on a baking sheet and chill in the fridge for 10 minutes.

6. Then, heat the oil in a large frying pan and fry the nuggets for 10–15 minutes until they are cooked through.

7. Remove excess oil by placing the nuggets on kitchen towel, then serve with oven chips and ketchup.

FRUITY SCONES

Makes twelve

You will need:
225 g (8 oz) self-raising flour
60 g (2 oz) soft butter or margarine
60 g (2 oz) caster sugar
60 g (2 oz) sultanas
150 ml (5 fl oz) milk

Method:

1. Put the flour in a mixing bowl and add the butter or margarine and the sugar.

2. Rub in with your fingers until the mixture has the consistency of breadcrumbs, then stir in the sultanas.

3. Pour in half of the milk and stir, then keep adding the milk until you have a soft dough.

4. Knead the dough lightly on a floured surface.

5. Roll out the dough to a thickness of 2 cm (0.75 inches). Cut into shapes with a floured round or bevel-edged cutter.

6. Place the shapes on a greased baking tray.

7. Bake in the oven at 230°C (450°F or Gas mark 8) for 10 minutes until golden. Then leave to cool on a wire rack.

'There's no place like home . . . except Grandma's!'
Author Unknown

HEALTHY FRUITY MUFFINS

MAKES TWELVE

You will need:
125 g (4.5 oz) self-raising flour
125 g (4.5 oz) wholemeal self-raising flour
40 g (1.5 oz) brown sugar
1 egg
3 tbsp rapeseed oil
200 ml (7 fl oz) milk
90 g (3 oz) raisins or dried mixed fruit
twelve muffin cases or a muffin tin

Method:

1. In a large bowl, mix both types of flour and the sugar together.

2. Add the egg and then slowly mix in the oil and the milk. Stir well.

3. Add the raisins or dried fruit and mix together.

4. Divide the mixture into twelve paper cases or a greased muffin tin.

5. Bake at 220°C (425°F or Gas mark 7) for 15–20 minutes.

TRIFLE POTS

MAKES FOUR

These are simple and involve no cooking, so they are great to make with younger children. They look scrumptious if made in glass dessert dishes, glass tumblers or large wine glasses.

You will need:
4 fairy cakes (shop-bought or previously made by you!)
2 tsp strawberry jam
2 tbsp fruit juice (raspberry or cranberry work best, but orange will do)
400 g (14 oz) fresh strawberries (quartered) or raspberries
300 ml (10 fl oz) custard
100 ml (3.5 fl oz) whipping cream
chocolate flakes or grated chocolate

Method:

1 Cut each fairy cake lengthways and sandwich back together with jam.

2 Divide each cake into four pieces and place at the bottom of each glass.

3 Add the fruit juice to moisten the sponge.

4 Divide the quartered strawberries or the whole raspberries between the four glasses.

5 Add a layer of custard.

6 Whip the cream until thick, then dollop on top of the custard.

7 Sprinkle with chocolate.

CHOCOLATE CHIP COOKIES

MAKES APPROXIMATELY TWENTY

Making cookies is guaranteed to win over the grandchildren. Not only are they fun to bake, but they're also delicious to eat, and you can almost certainly make enough for them to take home to Mum and Dad.

You will need:

50 g (1.75 oz) soft butter or margarine
100 g (3.5 oz) soft, light, brown sugar
1 tsp vanilla essence
1 egg
100 g (3.5 oz) plain flour
100 g (3.5 oz) chocolate chips

Method:

1. In a large bowl, beat the soft butter or margarine and sugar until pale and creamy.

2. Add the vanilla essence, egg and flour. Beat together well.

3. Stir in the chocolate chips.

4. Grease two baking sheets.

5. Spoon dollops of mixture onto the baking sheets, leaving space for the cookies to spread.

6. Bake the cookies at 180°C (350°F or Gas mark 4) for 8 minutes.

7. Remove from the oven and leave to cool for about 10 minutes, before transferring to a wire rack with a spatula.

BREAD AND BUTTER PUDDING

A traditional favourite and a great way of getting rid of slightly stale bread, the chances are that the children won't have tried it at home.

You will need:
6 medium slices of bread
75 g (2.5 oz) butter or margarine
50 g (1.75 oz) dried mixed fruit
40 g (1.5 oz) sugar
2 eggs
600 ml (1 pint) milk

Method:

1. Cut the crusts off the bread and butter each slice.

2. Cut into triangular quarters.

3. Arrange half the bread over the bottom of a shallow 2-pint (1.1-litre) dish and sprinkle over most of the fruit and half the sugar.

4. Top with the remaining bread, butter side up.

5. Beat the eggs, then add the milk, and beat again.

6. Pour over the mixture and sprinkle on the rest of the fruit and sugar.

7. Leave to stand for 20 minutes.

8. Bake the pudding at 180°C (350°F or Gas mark 4) for 45–50 minutes until firm and set.

9. Serve warm with cream, custard or vanilla ice cream.

CHRISTMAS PUDDING

FOR A TWO-PINT PUDDING BOWL

Making the Christmas pud used to be a treasured family ritual, but with so many nice puddings on the market, busy mums rarely feel the need to make their own. Few can beat this great Christmas pudding recipe, though, and it's lovely for the kids to know that they helped with the preparations for Christmas Day.

The pudding should be made several weeks before Christmas, to allow the fruit to mature, and it can be kept for up to a year.

You will need:

50 g (1.75 oz) self-raising flour
2 tsp mixed spice
pinch of salt
100 g (3.5 oz) breadcrumbs
100 g (3.5 oz) suet
75 g (2.5 oz) demerara sugar
50 g (1.75 oz) glacé cherries
350 g (12.5 oz) mixed fruit
25 g (1 oz) mixed peel
1 orange
1 lemon
1 apple
3 eggs
65 ml (2.25 fl oz) brandy or port

Method:

1 Combine the flour, spice and salt in a large bowl.

2 Add the breadcrumbs, suet and sugar. Stir together.

3 Quarter the cherries and add them to the mix, along with mixed fruit and peel.

4 Grate the rind of the orange and lemon into the bowl.

5 Cut the orange and lemon in half and squeeze the juice into the mix.

6 Core the apple and grate, then add to the mixture.

7 Beat the eggs and pour into the mixture along with the brandy or port.

8 Mix all the ingredients together well.

9 Grease a 2-pint (1-litre) pudding bowl and transfer the pudding mix into it.

10 Stir three times and make a wish! (This tradition is a favourite with the kids.)

11 Cover the top with foil or cloth and tie around the rim of the bowl with string.

12 Place a saucer (upside down) in the bottom of a large saucepan and put the pudding bowl on top.

⑬ Fill the pan with water to approximately 2.5 cm (1 inch) below the top of the bowl.

⑭ Boil for at least 8 hours, making sure the water level is constantly topped up. (You can divide boiling time to a couple of hours a day, if you prefer.) You can't over-boil, so don't worry if you heat it for longer than the recommended time.

⑮ Store in a cool cupboard and reheat on the day by boiling for an hour in a pan of water as above.

⑯ Serve with white sauce or brandy butter.

'What's so simple even a small child can manipulate it? Why, a grandmother, of course!'

AUTHOR UNKNOWN

Glamorous Grannies

JOANNA LUMLEY

Former model and proud granny Joanna Lumley is still absolutely fabulous even though she's in her sixties. The actress, who was born in 1946, was delighted when her grandchild Alice was born in 2003.

'Though I was a mother at twenty-one, being a grandmother makes the whole thing absolutely normal and gorgeous,' she has revealed. 'The relief, the joy of being a grandmother is wonderful.'

Still an immensely successful actress both on stage and screen, the *Ab Fab* star can always make time for the youngest member of the family. 'I babysit whenever I can,' she has said. 'Being a grand-mum is an immense privilege.'

But Joanna's granny status doesn't stop her being gorgeous and she regularly appears in polls of the most glamorous celebrities. She has put her good looks down to regular use of face cream, but she defends others who might resort to more drastic measures to stay young.

'I can't see any difference in having your hair dyed, your teeth fixed, your nose done, or your face smoothed out or lifted,' she has said.

'If people say, "Oh, you look old as the hills," you say, "I'm a grandmother, of course I look as old as the hills."'

JOANNA LUMLEY

SOPHIA LOREN

The sultry Italian star became a grandmother in 2007, the same year that she posed for a sexy Pirelli calendar – at the age of seventy-two. The stunning septuagenarian is the oldest woman to appear in the famous calendar and she looked fabulous.

'Of course, one wants to grow old gracefully,' she said. 'I like to take care of myself but I'm not afraid of getting wrinkles.'

In fact, she uses the same products as her tiny grandson to keep her skin soft and youthful. 'I like to use baby oil for cleansing my skin and baby shampoo to wash my hair, purely because they don't contain any harsh ingredients,' she explained. 'I never use any night cream on my face; just a little under-eye cream once I've removed my eye make-up.'

Family is Sophia's passion and, as a relatively late mother to her sons Carlo Jnr and Eduardo, she is thrilled to be a granny to baby Vittorio.

'He is the most beautiful baby in the world,' she remarked when he was five weeks old. 'He's wonderful and my son and his wife are so happy to have him. We just wait for him to say something and to do something for us . . . if you blow on his face he smiles.'

HONOR BLACKMAN

At the age of eighty, Honor Blackman looks younger than most sixty-year-olds and has a more active life than people half her age.

The former Bond Girl and star of *The Avengers* shuns the idea of retirement and spent the year before her eightieth birthday on a gruelling tour of her one-woman show, as well as a stint in *Cabaret* on the West End stage.

Honor, who wrote a beauty book called *How to Look and Feel Half Your Age For the Rest of Your Life*, says keeping active and interested is the key to staying young.

'People ask me, "Why do you last so well?" and I say, "Because I've always got an interest in life,"' she revealed. 'From the age of sixteen, I've always had something to do and somewhere to go.'

The mother of two became a granny at seventy-six and found herself with four grandchildren in three years. 'I thought I'd have one foot in the grave before I had one, and all of a sudden it was like the number eleven bus and they all came along at once!' she said. 'They're lovely.'

Like many grannies, Londoner Honor admits she would like her grandchildren to live nearer, since her daughter had moved to the country. 'It's lovely for the kids,' she explained. 'But it's upsetting for poor old grandmama.'

JOAN COLLINS

Actress Joan Collins is the archetypal independent granny. Although she adores her grandchildren, as soon as the first was born in 1998 she decided that she didn't want to be 'Granny' or 'Grandma'. Instead, her grandchildren call her 'DoDo'.

Now in her seventies, the *Dynasty* star is married to husband number five Percy Gibson, whom she met when she was sixty-eight and he was thirty-six.

'He loves my children and my baby grandchildren, so it works out really well,' she said during a TV interview with Larry King. 'We see the grandchildren quite often. And after a few weeks or a few days, we'd say, that's it, let's go back to having our own life and doing what we want to do and getting up when we want to, and not having to get up in the middle of the night.'

Joan is famed for her youthful looks and says a healthy and balanced diet has kept her young. 'I don't believe in eating junk and I protect my face all the time from the sun, even in the winter with base and make-up.'

Although she clearly takes care of herself, she's characteristically dismissive of the idea of ageing. 'Age, in my opinion, has no bearing at all. That is unless, of course, one happens to be a bottle of wine.'

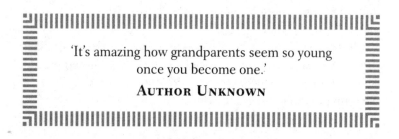

'It's amazing how grandparents seem so young once you become one.'

AUTHOR UNKNOWN

DAME SHIRLEY BASSEY

The Welsh diva, who is still packing huge stadiums after forty years at the top, is the epitome of glamour in a sequinned frock. But that didn't stop her showing up to perform at a wet and muddy Glastonbury festival in 2007, months after her seventieth birthday.

'You don't get older, you get better,' she has maintained, although she admits she works hard to look good. 'I had terrible skin as a young person,' she said. 'It's got better and better. And I work hard to look like this. I watch what I eat, I go to the gym every day, and I even work out before a show.'

Away from the glare of the spotlight, Dame Shirley has four grandchildren from daughter Sharon, although she doesn't get to do a lot of babysitting because she lives in the fittingly glamorous city of Monte Carlo.

GOLDIE HAWN

Blonde, bubbly and beautiful, it's hard to believe this movie star is a grandma, but in 2004, when grandson Ryder was born to actress daughter Kate Hudson, Goldie immediately shunned traditional names for the apt moniker 'Glamma'.

The star of *The First Wives' Club* and *Private Benjamin* attributes her looks to her regular intake of 'green fruit juice', along with the occasional carrot juice. Her miracle beverage apparently contains celery, parsley, kale and peppers. Yum!

Grandma Goldie also sticks to a strict exercise regime. 'I've never stopped working on my body,' she has said. 'I ride my bike up a mountain every day and I have to get on a running machine, do aerobics or dance daily.'

However, the Oscar-winning star also bemoaned the fate of ageing female actresses in Hollywood when she said, 'There are only three ages for women in Hollywood – Babe, District Attorney, and Driving Miss Daisy.'

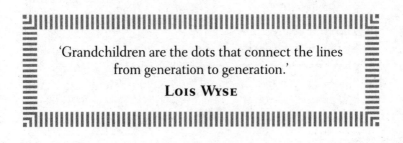

'Grandchildren are the dots that connect the lines from generation to generation.'
LOIS WYSE

Games to Play With the Grandkids

PICTURE CONSEQUENCES

Any number of players
Ages three and up

You will need paper and pens/pencils.

① Each player draws the head of an animal or person at the top of their piece of paper, making it as weird and funny as they like. Then they fold the paper over until only the bottom of the head is visible (as shown in the illustration).

② The paper is handed to the left and the next player adds a neck to the drawing. They fold the paper down to cover the neck, and pass it on to the person on their left.

③ This person draws a body of their choosing, folding it over as above and leaving an indication of where the legs should join on.

④ The next player adds the legs and feet, and folds the paper again, handing it to the left for the last time.

⑤ The strange creature is complete, so each player opens up their piece of paper to reveal the bizarre artistic results.

GRANNY, MAY I?

Three or more players
Ages three and up

Firstly, stand several steps away from the children with your back towards them. Then choose a child and give them an instruction, such as 'Molly, you may take two giant steps towards me.' She must then respond with 'Granny, may I?' and you can say 'Yes' or 'No'.

You can include different sized steps, such as giant, baby or normal, and can suggest silly styles like bunny hops and ballet steps. You can also make the children move backwards.

If the child forgets to ask 'Granny, may I?', he or she must go back to the start. The object of the game is to be the first child to reach Granny, and so the winner is the first one to touch you.

PAIRS (OR PELMANISM)

Two or more players
Ages four and up

You will need a pack of ordinary cards or a child's 'Snap' deck.

1. Shuffle the pack and spread the cards out, face down, on a table or floor.

2. Starting with the youngest child, each player turns over two cards. If they match, the player keeps the cards and has another go. If they are not a pair, all players try to remember what was on each card, and the cards are turned over once more.

3 The next player then turns over two cards and looks for a pair. Each pair found means the player has an extra turn.

4 The game is over when all the cards have been picked up, and the winner is the person with the most pairs.

IN THE MANNER OF THE WORD

Two or more players
Ages five and up

This is an old parlour game that can be played anywhere and needs no equipment, but the more people involved the better.

1 One person is sent outside the room and the other players (or player) decide on an adverb, such as 'angrily' or 'sadly'.

2 The excluded person is then called back into the room and asks the rest of the party to perform specific acts 'in the manner of the word.' For example, if the word is 'angrily', she could say to one player 'Pick up that book' and the player would pick up the book in an aggressive and angry manner. She could then ask the next player to tell her the time, which would also be done in a cross way.

3 The player continues to ask others to perform acts until he or she has guessed the word.

It is not necessary to score this game, but if you want to you could award points for the number of 'acts' requested before the correct guess, and the winner would be the person with the least points. You can also play this game in teams if there are a large number of people present.

TELEGRAMS

Three or more players
Ages five and up

You will need pens and paper and a timer or watch with a second hand.

Each player picks a letter, all of which are written in a column down the left-hand side of your paper. If there are a small number of people playing, it may be necessary to go round two or three times as you need a minimum of eight letters.

When all the letters are written down, players have two minutes to come up with a funny message in the style of a telegram, using the chosen letters to begin each word.

For example, if you had the letters M O W H S H T C, the telegram might read:

> Mum's
> On
> Way
> Home
> Stop
> Hide
> The
> Cat

Telegrams is not a competitive game, but can still provide plenty of laughs. Mind you, in the era of e-mails and text messages, the old-fashioned concept of a telegram might need some explaining!

BATTLESHIPS

Two players
Ages seven and up

There are expensive electronic versions of this on the market, but you can still play it with paper and a pencil. You could use graph paper or make your own with a ruler, pencil and paper.

You will need four square grids of ten squares by ten. The squares are numbered 1–10 along the bottom and lettered from A–J up the left-hand side.

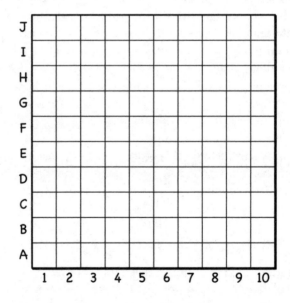

Each player has an allocation of five ships, which each take up a different number of spaces. (You can vary the allocation if you wish.) They are:

Type of ship	Size (number of spaces)
Aircraft Carrier	5
Battleship	4
Submarine	3
Destroyer	3
PT Boat	2

Keeping his grids hidden from the opponent, each player plots his ships on one of his grids and keeps the other one to record his 'shots'. The ships must be arranged horizontally or vertically, not diagonally, and must not overlap.

When the ships are positioned, players take it in turn to take shots by identifying a square on his opponent's grid, e.g. C2. If the opponent has a ship in the square, he must say 'hit'. If not he will say 'miss'.

Players record their own shots on their spare grid and their opponent's shots on their main grid.

A ship is sunk when each of the squares it occupies have been hit. The player must then tell the opponent which of his ships has been scuppered, e.g. 'You've sunk my Battleship.'

The first player to sink all his opponent's ships is the winner.

'A grandmother is a babysitter who watches the kids instead of the television.'

AUTHOR UNKNOWN

Growing Old Disgracefully

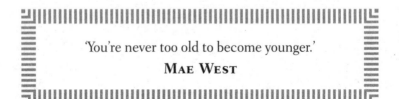

'You're never too old to become younger.'
MAE WEST

The traditional image of a granny is a white-haired old lady who sits in her favourite chair knitting and telling stories of the good old days. But the twenty-first-century gran is a very different creature.

You are more likely to find her running around the garden playing football with her grandchildren or competing in endless games of snap than knitting bootees. Chances are Granny has a career or has retired from one, and having been a busy mum herself she is enjoying the time that she gets to spend with her grandchildren.

As a new millennium granny, you're full of surprises! So the next time your children and grandchildren start to take you for granted, here are a few things you might want to do to make them stop and take notice:

* learn to fly a plane

* take up surfing (the waves rather than the web)

* have some plastic surgery

* book a naturist holiday

* join a singles' club (but only if you are!)

* dye your hair shocking pink

* go backpacking around the world

* buy a sports car

THINGS MODERN-DAY GRANNIES HAVE SWAPPED . . .

* curlers for hair straighteners

* crimplene for denim

* baking bread for being a breadwinner

* housework for house parties

* sewing for surfing the net

* petit point for Pilates

* sherry for Shiraz

* granny glasses for contact lenses

HOBBIES TO IMPRESS
THE GRANDCHILDREN

* dance classes

* canoeing

* sailing

* amateur dramatics

* buying and selling on Internet auction sites

* guitar lessons

* carpentry

* making jewellery

* windsurfing

* playing computer games on the latest console

* beekeeping

* rock climbing

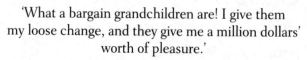

'What a bargain grandchildren are! I give them
my loose change, and they give me a million dollars'
worth of pleasure.'
GENE PERRET

Don't Call Me Grandma!

You may be celebrating grandmotherhood, but that doesn't mean you feel old enough to be called Grandma or Granny. After all, the average age of a new grandparent is only forty-nine in the UK and forty-seven in the US, so you're not ready for the crocheted shawl and rocking chair just yet.

An increasing number of new grandparents are shunning the traditional names, including celebrities such as Goldie Hawn, who opted for Glamma. Being called by your first name is not advisable, however, as it can send confusing messages to the child and make them unsure of your relationship with them.

Some favoured alternatives include Nanna, Nanny, Grammy, Gammy and Grams. But if you fancy something a little bit different, why not try some foreign-language options:

* Babka – Polish

* Lola – Filipino

* Mémé – French

* Mummo – Finnish

* Nonna – Italian

* Oma – German

* Sobo – Japanese

* Ugogo – Zulu

Or how about 'Moogie', used in sci-fi TV shows *Star Trek* and *Deep Space Nine*?

Perfect Present Buying

The art of buying the perfect gift for your grandchildren is a fine balancing act. Always remember that, as well as pleasing the recipient of the gift, you must avoid annoying the parents, who will have to live with the consequences of your choice.

Before picking up the biggest, plastic, electronic toy in the store, imagine a scene in your son or daughter's house, after the toy has been opened, and ask yourself the following important questions:

* Do they have the space for it?

* Where will they put it?

* Is it easy to assemble/dismantle?

* Does it go back in the box?

* Has he/she got a million similar things?

* Is it too noisy?

As a golden rule, parents tend to like presents that are educational, fun, reasonably small and won't be discarded or fall apart within days.

BEST BABY PRESENTS

When the bundle of joy is on the way, the world seems to be awash with the cutest cuddly toys but, as a grandparent, it pays to think practical. Ask your children what they would like you to buy and tell them how much you want to spend – that way they'll know whether you'll stretch to paying for a car seat or pushchair, or if you just want to buy some clothes. Here are some suggestions that should win the vote of potential parents.

Baby basket

Fill a huge basket with nappies, wipes and nappy sacks as well as baby bubble bath and soap, and a few beauty treats for the new mum. Not only will it be appreciated, but it will save them a lot of money.

Sterilizer

Most new mums need one, but check first that they haven't already got one.

Bedding

A pretty blanket for baby is always useful and you could throw in a few cot sheets too.

Activity centre for the cot

Great for stimulating babies when they are old enough to push buttons and ring bells.

Baby gym

The baby lies on a mat underneath two arches with activities suspended from them. It'll keep him or her amused for hours.

Inflatable ring

These fabric-covered rubber rings are invaluable when baby is almost ready to sit up but can't do so without falling over.

Lullaby night light

There are some great baby lights on the market that throw interesting shapes on the walls and ceiling.

Interactive cuddly toy

If you do want to buy something cute and cuddly, make it an electronic toy that teaches baby to press buttons to hear music and nursery rhymes.

Bouncing cradle

These hold the baby safely while they gently bounce. Babies love them!

Children's savings bonds/account

Grandmothers can build up a nestegg for their grandchildren by buying bonds or opening a savings account in their name, and paying in money on birthdays or at Christmas. The kids will be thrilled when they're old enough to make use of Granny's generous gift.

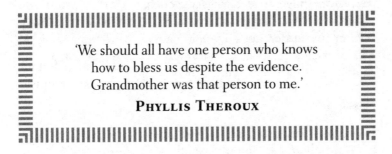

'We should all have one person who knows
how to bless us despite the evidence.
Grandmother was that person to me.'
PHYLLIS THEROUX

WORST BABY PRESENTS

Cuddly toys

As a grandmother it is your duty NEVER to add to the cuddly toy mountain that inevitably accumulates in every small child's bedroom!

Newborn baby clothes

If you do want to buy baby clothes, never buy newborn size. Lots of other people will, so be practical. In six to nine months, no one will be buying gifts, so choose outfits for then, but make sure you take season into account. It's no good buying a winter coat for a 6–9-month-old if your grandchild is born in December!

Designer clothes

There really is no point in buying Dolce & Gabbana tops for a person who is going to dribble sour milk and orange baby food down them all day.

Shoes

There are expensive shoes and trainers on the market for babies but, until they are at least six months old, they are pretty pointless and also not good for a child's feet. Inexpensive fabric booties (or knitted ones if you are a really traditional granny) will keep their feet warm. Let's face it, they're not going to be running a marathon any time soon.

Earrings

Babies are perfectly formed little human beings and putting holes in their ears merely spoils that natural perfection. Goodness only knows they'll be imperfect teenagers before you know it.

MP3 player

Not even for nursery rhymes . . .

BEST PRESENTS FOR OLDER CHILDREN

Wooden fort or dolls' house

As long as your son or daughter has room indoors, these are still wonderful toys. It also solves present buying for the future, as there'll always be a list of new things to add.

White board

Complete with wipe-clean marker pens, a drawing board makes a wonderful gift and will save on the mound of paper and endless paintings that mums are not supposed to throw away.

PC game

Most families have a computer and there are hundreds of games available that are educational as well as fun. A PC game tends to cost a lot less than those that go with the popular consoles, too.

Building bricks

Lego and its equivalents are still very popular with kids and the versatility of building bricks means they'll never get bored.

Sports equipment

If the children have a garden, new sporting gear encourages them to be active. Cricket sets, golf sets and badminton sets are widely available in children's sizes and you can't go wrong with a football, whatever age and sex the kids are.

Watch

For children over five, a watch is a great gift as it will encourage your grandchild to tell the time.

Art set

Pens, pencils and paints are always running out, so the big sets of art materials make a perfect, inexpensive gift.

Bike

If your budget can stretch to it, a bicycle is most likely to be welcomed by both adult and child. Who doesn't like the idea of a new bike?

Books

You can never have too many.

Electronic reading system

Perfect for pre-school learning, although not cheap.

WORST PRESENTS FOR OLDER CHILDREN

Crying baby doll

Unless it comes with an off switch and your grandchild only plays with it in her bedroom!

High-maintenance toys

It's all very well buying your little darlings the latest remote-control car or robotic dinosaur, but if the remote requires four batteries and the toy another six, don't. You might provide the batteries the first time round but, three days later, when they run out, it will be down to the parents to keep replacing them.

Drum kit

Or a drum of any kind.

Huge plastic garage or fire station etc.

Every birthday and Christmas, parents despair at the biggest parcels in the pile. When opened they produce endless plastic bits that will take three hours to assemble, before turning into a plastic folly, standing two feet high, never to be put away again.

Guns

Boys may well gravitate towards playing with guns on their own, but these days many parents shy away from providing them. If so, they won't thank you for buying him a semi-automatic so he can pretend to murder his sister!

A puppy

Not unless you've had the all-clear from their parents first!

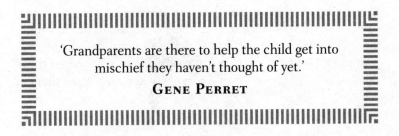

'Grandparents are there to help the child get into mischief they haven't thought of yet.'
GENE PERRET

Granny's Lotions and Potions

Traditional remedies are passed down from generation to generation, but how many of them really work? Here are the scientific explanations behind some of the age-old cures for everyday ills that are really effective.

Wasp and bee stings

Forget your expensive sting ointments: Granny knows best when it comes to stings. Bees and ants have acidic stings, which means an alkali is needed to neutralize it. For this reason the best treatment for a bee sting is bicarbonate of soda or even unperfumed soap. Conversely, the wasp's sting is alkaline, so the best thing for those is an acid, such as vinegar.

If you find it difficult to remember which sting needs which treatment, just tell yourself 'Bee' for Bicarbonate.

Nettle stings

Everyone knows that dock leaves are the answer to nettle stings, but do you know why? Like the bee sting, the pain from a nettle rash is caused by a reaction to an acidic substance. The dock leaf contains an alkali and therefore soothes the pain away. It can also be used on bee and ant stings.

Toothache

Chewing cloves or using clove oil has long been regarded as a great cure for toothache. The reason it works is due to the large concentration of a substance called eugenol, which has antimicrobial properties that restricts the growth of bacteria and viruses. It is also a mild anaesthetic, which helps to relieve the pain.

To cure a bout of toothache, one or two cloves should be chewed, or an oil of cloves product rubbed on the gums. Be aware, though, that full-strength oil of cloves should not be used, as it can damage nerves. It's best to check with a pharmacist before buying a product containing oil of cloves.

Fresh figs also contain an anti-inflammatory agent, and when rubbed on the gums they are a good alternative cure for young children if clove products are too bitter.

Hayfever

Honey from local bees is said to be the natural answer to the yearly onslaught of hayfever. Sufferers should take one spoonful of honey a day, all year round, which delivers a tiny dose of the pollen from their immediate area. This way the body can build a resistance to the pollen that triggers an attack, so that when spring arrives it doesn't react so violently.

Alternatively, you could try some nettle soup. As well as being an excellent source of calcium, magnesium, iron and vitamins, it is an ancient cure for hayfever. It contains anti-immune-boosting proteins and an anti-inflammatory agent that acts as an antihistamine. Cook in place of spinach in soups and casseroles, or buy some nettle tea, and the itchy eyes and sneezing should clear up.

(Caution: nettles are not suitable for anyone taking anti-coagulant medication.)

Cuts

You may have heard of rubbing salt in wounds (not recommended, obviously), but what about pepper? Black pepper placed directly on an external cut will stop bleeding and, amazingly, it doesn't sting. Cayenne pepper is also effective. If the cut is deep, medical help should always be sought, but the pepper will stem the bleeding in the meantime, especially if you pack the wound.

Cayenne can also be used to stop nosebleeds, and a poultice of the pepper wrapped around a wound is also thought to reduce scarring.

Earwax

A child's ear is a delicate instrument and a build-up of wax might make them want to dig their fingers inside, thereby causing damage. Olive oil is a simple, cheap and effective way of clearing wax. Warm some olive oil to body temperature and then, using a pipette, put one or two drops into the ear. Repeat once or twice a day until the wax clears.

(Caution: if the child is suffering any discomfort or pain, do not put drops in, but, rather, see a doctor.)

Olive oil is also a perfect remedy for dry skin in babies. Rather than using manufactured baby oil, rub a few drops of olive oil between your palms and then smooth over baby's skin.

Colds and sinusitis

If your grandchild is all snuffly and bunged up, a home-made lemonade will give them a lift. Dissolve a teaspoon of honey in a mug of hot water and add the juice of four lemons and one orange (optional). Then top up with cold water and refrigerate.

The drink helps ease congestion by cutting mucus production and also provides a boost of vitamin C, which helps fight the cold. This is a child-friendly, non-alcoholic version of the traditional hot toddy.

Insomnia

Every granny knows that lavender is a natural promoter of sleep so, if your grandchildren are staying over while mum and dad are out enjoying themselves, a drop of lavender oil on a pillow, or in the bedtime bath, might help them to drop off.

It Never Did Us Any Harm...

If you were brought up on a daily dose of syrup of figs, you might want to know if the age-old cure-alls did you more harm than good. Were your parents misled or could the youth of today still benefit from the odd dose of a foul-tasting formula?

Cod liver oil

The long-held belief that fish oil is good for growing brains seems to have been borne out by recent research. Fish oils contain omega-3 fatty acids, which are important for nerve function, and children with low omega-3 levels in their body have been found to be more likely to be hyperactive and display behavioural problems. Some studies have shown that supplements can help children with dyslexia and attention-deficit disorders.

Omega-3s can be found in a natural diet, of course, with oily fish such as sardines, mackerel and salmon the best providers. The UK's Food Standards Agency recommends two portions of fish a week. Given that fish is not the favourite food of most kids, however, a supplement might be an idea. These days, health food shops do special packs for kids, so no need for any howls of protest at the fishy spoonful proffered after breakfast!

Castor oil

Grannies through the centuries have used a dose of castor oil to flush out the system, and it certainly does have purgative properties. However, as its laxative powers are so strong, it is no longer recommended for children under twelve or for prolonged use. After all, it is also used as a fuel for lamps in India, and some evil regimes have been known to use it as a form of torture . . .

Syrup of figs

Figs are known for their mild, laxative properties and the syrup made from the fruit is a traditional cure for constipation. Originating from natural products, the liquid is suitable for children and is still available, and effective, today. The taste is an acquired one, however, so getting a fussy child to swallow a dose isn't always easy.

Chicken soup

The loveliest and most soothing of remedies for a child with a cold is grandma's home-made chicken soup – even if grandma has never made it before! The soup helps to boost the immune system, slows down the production of mucus and provides much needed nutrition. So get cooking!

'A grandparent has the wisdom of long experience and the love of an understanding heart.'

AUTHOR UNKNOWN

How to Be a Hands-off Granny

Obviously you're delighted to have a grandchild at last but, if you're dreading the thought of being left holding the baby too often, here are some tips on keeping babysitting chores at bay.

* Move as far away from your children as you can, but try not to make it somewhere that's too attractive to visit, like a luxury villa in Spain.

* Take to throwing wild parties and having unsuitable characters hanging around your house.

* Take up smoking – a sure-fire way to alienate most modern parents.

* Buy a Rottweiler.

* Buy a motorbike and join the local branch of the Hell's Angels.

* Feign incompetence by putting the baby's nappies on back to front and filling their milk bottles with fizzy pop.

* Get a job with really unsociable hours.

* Just say no!

Granny's Arts and Crafts

A CARD FOR ALL OCCASIONS

Discount shops and certain supermarkets sell packs of coloured cardboard and paper, so it is worth investing in a few of these if you have grandchildren.

A4 packs are the ideal size for making greeting cards and, as you will remember from your own kids, a home-made Mother's Day card is the best sort.

Coloured card always looks pretty, but make sure it's not too dark as it will be more difficult to write and draw on.

Patchwork heart

This is a great card design because it requires little artistic skill and even very young children can help.

You will need:
a thin piece of A4 card
scraps of wrapping paper, magazine pages,
foil and/or crêpe paper
scissors
craft glue
glitter (optional)

1 Start by folding the two shorter edges of the A4 card together to create a greetings-card shape.

2 On the front of the card, draw a large heart. Make sure it's in the centre and leave space at the top for the word MUM, which should be in big letters.

3 Cut up scraps of wrapping paper, foil, crêpe paper and magazine pages featuring attractive designs. Make sure that the scissors are not too sharp if your grandchild is doing the cutting, and keep a beady eye on him or her at all times.

4 Cover the heart with glue and get your grandchild to stick the paper scraps within the heart, making sure that they don't go over the edge and distort the shape.

5 At the top of the page write MUM in block letters and fill in with glue.

6 Over a newspaper, sprinkle glitter over the top of the card and then shake off the excess, leaving behind a sparkling 'MUM'.

7 Write your message inside.

Caution: not all mums will appreciate a card that spreads glitter all over the house, so the word 'MUM' could be coloured in with paints or pens instead. However, if you feel like wreaking revenge for all the time you spent hoovering glitter from the furniture when your own kids were young, sprinkle away!

Crêpe-paper creation

Using pieces of different coloured crêpe paper, you and your grandchild can make a beautifully decorated card suitable for any occasion.

1 Fold the card as in the previous step one, and get your grandchild to draw a picture on the front. It could be a scene of the whole family, of mum or of a bunch of flowers.

2 Put blobs of glue in the places where you want to stick the crêpe paper, e.g. the clothes of family figures, petals of flowers or as individual flowers in a garden.

3 Screw up the scraps of different coloured crêpe paper into tiny balls and stick on to the picture.

4 When the glue has dried, colour in the remaining picture and write your message.

✳ ✳ ✳

Father's Day shirt-and-tie card

This is a really effective and simple card for Father's Day, and the message can be hidden under the tie.

You will need:
1 sheet of thick A4 card or a cereal box
scissors
2 sheets of white A4 paper
glue
construction paper or thick card for the tie
colouring pens or crayons
ruler

❶ Cut the piece of card (or one side of the cereal box) so that it measures 12.5 cm (5 inches) by 21 cm (8 inches).

❷ Take a sheet of white paper and place it down horizontally. Then place the card in the centre of the white paper vertically.

❸ Fold the white paper over the card so that it covers it completely, and glue it down on the back.

❹ To create a collar effect on the shirt, cut the top of the card into an 'M' shape, then fold down the two peaks.

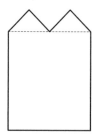

❺ Next, using the construction paper or thick card, cut out a tie shape.

❻ Use felt-tip pens or crayons to design a funky pattern on the tie.

7 Glue the top of the tie to the card, ensuring that the rest of the tie can move up and down freely.

8 Glue the collar flaps down on to the shirt.

9 Write a message on the underside of the tie e.g. 'Happy Father's Day!' or 'To The World's Best Dad!'

10 Now lift the tie and draw a straight line down the middle of the front of the shirt. You can then draw on some buttons and colour them in.

11 You could also draw a pocket on either side of the tie.

12 To make the card stand up by itself, cut another piece of card into a rectangle measuring 12.5 cm (5 inches) by 5 cm (2 inches). Measure 2 cm (0.75 inch) from the edge, fold the card over and glue the bent part onto the back of your card to help to keep it upright.

Pop-up Easter card

Perfect for Easter, this clever card is easy to make, lots of fun and is certain to keep the grandkids amused, especially younger ones.

You will need:
2 pieces of thin A4 card (or very thick paper)
in different colours
glue
scissors
colouring pens, pencils or crayons

1. Fold one piece of card in half, then, midway down the card, cut a line of about 5 cm (2 inches) from the left-hand crease.

2. Fold back each of the flaps to make two triangles, thereby making a large triangular hole at the spine.

3. Run your nails along the triangle edges to make sure the creases are sharp.

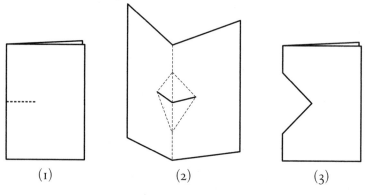

(1)   (2)   (3)

4. Straighten the triangles and open the card about halfway (resting it on one's knees is a good way to keep it from laying flat).

5 Push one of the triangles through the hole and pinch to make it stand up. Repeat with the other triangle.

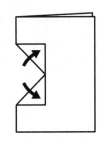

6 Close the card and push down on the folds to make them well creased. When opened, you should now have a pop-up beak.

7 Fold the second piece of card in half, glue around the inside edges, and stick to the back of the pop-up card, making sure the glue does not go near the beak.

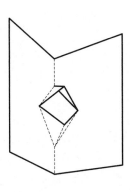

8 Next you can have some fun drawing a bird's face around the beak and decorating the front of your card as you wish, perhaps adding an Easter message and some spring flowers.

3-D Christmas tree card

What better way to prepare for Christmas than to help the grandkids create a unique 3-D tree card, adorned with colourful decorations.

You will need:
1 sheet of paper or thin card
green card
brown card
red card
paint, beads, silver foil, gold and silver
star stickers, glitter and sequins etc.
glue

1 Using the paper or thin card, make the template by cutting a rectangle measuring 12 cm (5 inches) by 20 cm (8 inches). Fold in half vertically to make a width of 6 cm (2.5 inches).

2 Draw three horizontal lines to divide the card into four equal sections, each with a height of 5 cm (2 inches).

3 The top three sections will form the main part of the tree. Draw a steep diagonal line from the top of the crease to a third of the way across the first line. Then draw two more staggered diagonal lines underneath to form the basic shape (see diagram).

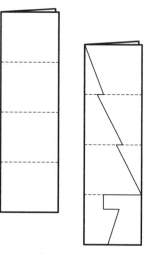

4 Next, draw the trunk and container shape in the bottom section.

5 Carefully cut out the shape across the fold and open it up.

6 Using this template, place over the green card and cut out two identical shapes.

7 Decorate the green trees with your silver foil, sequins, bead and paint. Add some glitter if you like. Cover the trunk with a small piece of brown card and the container with some of the red card.

8 When the decorations have dried, cut a 10-cm (4-inch) slit down the centre of one of the trees from the top. Then, from the bottom of the other tree, cut another 10-cm (4-inch) slit.

9 Slide the two trees together to form a cross at the base.

10 Add a gold or silver foil star sticker at the top to hold in place.

You can put the finishing touches to your pretty 3-D Christmas tree by writing a message on the container or hanging a Yuletide message off the tree itself.

Granny Anecdotes

TRUE STORIES
FROM REAL-LIFE GRANNYHOOD

Joe, aged five, was asked what he thought grandparents were for. This was his reply:

> My Grandma is for setting the table.
> My Grandad Gerry is for playing.
> My Granny is for doing puzzles on the floor.
> My Grandad Maurice is for sitting in the garden reading a newspaper.

As her parents and grandparents debated the lack of modern history taught in schools these days, eight-year-old Georgia sat listening intently.

Eventually her grandma turned to her and said, 'Do you know who Churchill is?'

'Of course I do,' she replied, indignantly. 'He's the nodding dog in the insurance advert!'

* * *

Grandma Kath took her three-year-old grandchild Louise to the toilets at a crowded seaside resort. As the queue for the ladies' loos was so long, she decided to share Louise's cubicle and spend a penny herself.

As she pulled her trousers down, Louise piped up, in her loudest voice, 'Grandma, why do you wear such big knickers?'

Poor Grandma has never left a public convenience so quickly!

* * *

Great-grandmother Dorothy was chatting to her grown-up granddaughter about keeping in touch with friends.

'I'm having trouble getting in touch with people at the moment,' lamented her granddaughter. 'I've lost my address book and I can't find it anywhere.'

'Never mind dear,' said Dorothy helpfully. 'You can have mine!'

* * *

Hillary was looking after her young grandchild when he ran in from the garden.

'Granny, there's a big grey bird outside, with a green neck,' gushed the lad.

'Is it a wood pigeon?' asked Hillary.

'No,' replied the puzzled boy. 'It's a real one!'

Celebrities and Their Grandmothers

50 Cent's soft side

Rapper 50 Cent may have a hard-man image, but he's devoted to his granny! Born Curtis James Jackson III, '50' was taken in by his grandma after his mother died when he was only eight. However, despite her best efforts, his gran couldn't keep young Curtis on the straight and narrow, and he took up drug dealing and ran with gangs from an early age. He later reflected, 'I became two people – one was the hardcore drug dealer in the day, and the other was my grandmother's baby by night.'

As his gangster lifestyle caught up with him, the young rapper was shot nine times outside his grandmother's house, while his own baby son slept inside. With stints in jail and a troubled past behind him, 50 Cent is now one of the bestselling rap artists in the world, and still remains very close to his grandma.

He used some of his newfound riches to buy her a new house, and, when he was lacking inspiration for his album *Curtis*, he returned to her old home, a cramped basement in Queen's, New York.

'I wrote and recorded lyrics for this album at my grandmother's house again,' he said on its release. 'I went back in the basement, where you have to bend down, the ceiling is so low, where I wrote (hit album) *Get Rich Or Die Tryin'*. Being in that environment helped me remember things . . .'

Style guru

Actress Rosario Dawson thinks her grandmother is so cool that she swaps clothes with her! The beautiful star of *Sin City* regularly raids her grandmother's wardrobe and shares the odd beer with her too.

'My grandmother just turned seventy-one,' she explained. 'We drink Bud and hang out. Normally I wear her clothes. We're the exact same size, so it works out really well.

'She's from Puerto Rico and her English is still not 100 per cent. She'll be like "Rosario, look at the alligator on the window" and it's actually a lizard. Or she'll say, "Look at the carpenter bird" and it will be a woodpecker. It's really cute stuff. It's adorable. I love her!'

Message from beyond

US actress Jennifer Love Hewitt believes she was contacted by her dead grandmother while she was making a television show. The star of *I Know What You Did Last Summer* was filming *Ghost Whisperer* at the time, which is a show that revolves around James Van Praagh and Mary Ann Winkowski, two American mediums who have convinced Jennifer that it is possible to contact the dead.

One night, during a session directed by Van Praagh, she says her dead grandmother made herself known. 'We had an evening with James where he did this thing and my grandmother came through,' she revealed. 'She just wanted to say hello and tell me that she was looking out for me. It was really nice.'

Where there's a Will . . .

Before marrying Jada Pinkett-Smith, comic actor Will Smith took her to meet his grandmother, but things didn't go well . . .

'When I met Will's grandmother it was pretty embarrassing,' a cringing Jada once recalled. 'I walked in and she had just finished watching *Jason's Lyric* – I have a pretty explicit love scene in that movie. I walked in and Will says, "G.D., this is Jada."

'She kind of looked at me and said, "I just don't know why young people feel like they gotta take their clothes off all the time." I looked at Will, like, "Is this a joke?". . . I can look at it now and think it's pretty funny, but [at the time] I was really upset.'

Guess who recommended the film to dear old Grandma – Will, of course!

Justin Trousersnake?

Soon after her 2003 break-up with pop star Justin Timberlake, Britney Spears opened her heart on MTV. Admitting that she was 'just a little bitter', the singer shocked viewers by emphasizing the words 'just' and 'little', and indicating a short length with her thumb and finger.

The implication about Justin's manhood had one lady jumping to his defence – his seventy-year-old grandmother Sadie Bomar. 'I helped raise him,' she declared, 'and I can assure you there is nothing wrong with him.'

Ironically, given Britney's cheeky intimation, his nickname in many tabloids has been Justin Trousersnake!

Who Shot Granny?

Actor and comedian Tim Allen was a bit of a tearaway as a child – and poor granny had a scar to prove it.

'I sold seeds door-to-door and I got one of those Daisy pumps (air rifles),' Allen remembered. 'It was almost a pellet gun. What you want is a bored, armed eleven-year-old running around in the back yard!

'They had a little target you could shoot at – ping, ping, ping, ping. That's so boring really quick, so I looked around for something moving – "Boy, look at grandma over there." I'm not proud of it, but I shot her in the back of the leg. I took her down!'

Granny's shame

Eva Longoria was delighted to win the role of sexy Gabrielle Solis in *Desperate Housewives*, but her grandmother was less than impressed. In fact, she even stopped talking to the actress altogether.

'She is an old, traditional Mexican grandma,' explained the actress. 'She doesn't really get the whole acting thing. She doesn't understand the profession of acting. She was like, "What were you doing on TV with that boy!" I told her, "Grandma, It's fake, it's not real."

'I tried to think of every adjective I could think of. So I said, "It's a lie." And she said, "Why are you lying! That's worse!"'

Diddy little twins

Hip-hop celebrity P. Diddy honoured two precious grand-mothers when he and girlfriend Kim Porter had their twin girls in December 2006. The babies were named Jessie James and D'Lila Star after the star's grandma Jessie Smalls and Kim's gran Lila Star.

'In honour of the two people to have incredibly impacted mine and Kim's lives,' said the singer, 'we're proud to announce that we are naming the twins after our beloved grandmothers.'

Ahhhhh!

'Grandmother-grandchild relationships are simple. Grandmas are short on criticism and long on love.'

AUTHOR UNKNOWN

Green-fingered Granny

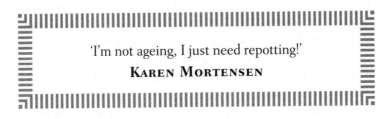
Gardening is a wonderful thing to do with your grandchildren and can be both fun and educational for them too.

If you have room, set aside a little part of a flower bed for them to grow plants that they've chosen themselves. If space is limited, help them to plant a container or window box with their favourite flowers.

Start them off young; garden centres and toy shops do delightful gardening sets for tiny hands. Invest in a mini watering can so that even a toddler can join in the fun, watering your garden or containers for you as a play activity.

PLANTS

The plants you choose will depend on many factors. Take into consideration the space you have, climate conditions and whether the site is sunny, shady or partly in the shade.

If your grandchildren are regular visitors they will be able to tend their plants and will doubtless be excited to see the progress of their own little patch every time they come. If visits are rare, try to choose plants that will last throughout the year, such as rose bushes or shrubs, rather than those that flower briefly, like daffodils. That way the grandchildren won't be disappointed to find they have missed seeing their flowers in full bloom.

Dangerous plants

Always check that the plants you choose to grow are not poisonous to young children. Make sure that you teach the children *never* to put anything from the garden in their mouth without asking a grown-up first.

This is a list of the most common plants to avoid in the garden, but always check when buying any new plants that they are safe for young children:

Foxgloves	Bleeding heart
Rhubarb	Wisteria
Daphne	Lily-of-the-valley
Larkspur	Oleander
Holly	Ivy
Poppies	Fuchsia

SUMMER COLOUR

Here are a few suggestions for plants that are perfect for introducing a child to the delights of gardening. Of course there are many more on the market, and you may have your own favourites to share with your grandchildren.

For shady areas

Fuchsias and astilbes are ideal for containers and beds in a shady area, and bring lots of lovely colour when they flower. Fuchsias bloom between August and October, and astilbes blossom from June to August. Begonias make a colourful splash in the summer too, but be sure to select the right variety as many are houseplants. Cyclamen also provide ground cover and a nice dash of colour.

For greenery, ferns and hostas are best for shady spots.

For sunny areas

The choice of flowers for sunny areas is endless, but children's favourites include pansies, sweet peas, lilies and daisies. Roses are also really popular, and come in a huge range of colours and varieties. Patio roses are wonderful if you want to plant in containers, and a small rose bush brightens up a bed beautifully. If you have a blank wall, a climbing rose in a pot or a bed looks lovely. Sunflowers are fabulous to grow in a sheltered sunny spot and kids love to see how tall their bloom will grow.

For greenery, herbs are the perfect plant to grow in the sun. Try thyme, parsley or mint. Not only are they decorative, but they can be useful when cooking, too.

SPRING'S ETERNAL

Create a container or a small bed that will produce new flowers throughout the spring. Planting bulbs is one of the easiest ways for children to start gardening and, if you plant in the autumn, you can produce a spectacular spring display.

Daffodils, tulips and crocuses are all great plants to start with. However, daffodil bulbs are poisonous if eaten, so make sure that young children are watched at all times while planting and that they wash their hands thoroughly after handling them.

Choose flower varieties that will blossom in early spring (crocuses and daffodils), mid-spring (hyacinths) and late spring (tulips). Plant them in good soil and compost, and await the fabulous results.

HANGING BASKETS

Any outside area can be brightened up with a spring and summer basket. They are readily available cheaply online or from garden centres, as well as some supermarkets and discount shops.

If the basket is bought unlined, you will need to line it with some commercial product or with a circle of plastic sheeting (e.g. cut from a compost bag). Moss can be put underneath the sheeting to improve the look of the bottom of the basket.

If using plastic, make sure you cut three slits in the lining (measuring about 2.5 cm or 1 inch) to allow excess water to escape. Plan how you're going to arrange your basket first, putting taller bedding plants in the centre and trailing plants on the outside. Ideal plants for hanging baskets are trailing fuchsias, busy Lizzies, trailing geraniums and lobelias. For the top, bush geraniums, petunias and fuchsias are among the best, although there are plenty of different varieties.

When you've lined your basket, fill it to halfway with a soil-based compost and add water-retention granules to help the plants along. Add the side plants (lobelias, trailing geraniums, etc.) by making a small hole in the liner or moss and inserting the plant, root first, through it, making sure that the roots reach the compost.

The next step is to fill up the basket with compost to about 2.5 cm (1 inch) from the top, leaving a slight slope down towards the centre, then plant your other varieties. Start at the centre and work your way out, firming each plant in. Fill any gaps with border plants such as lobelias and petunias, and use trailing varieties for the edges.

The basket can be planted in early spring, but do not put outside until the last frost has gone. Ensure that the basket is watered daily.

If you have nowhere to hang a basket, wall planters (containers that are nailed or screwed to the wall) are a cheap and pretty alternative.

GROWING VEGETABLES

You don't have to have a huge garden to grow your own produce. Troughs, tubs, window boxes and grow bags are all space-saving alternatives you can use to grow your own organic fruit and veg, and the children will be keen to try something healthy if they have had a hand in growing it.

Choose a food that you will enjoy eating fresh and that you will want to eat often. Salad leaves are a good choice – home-grown rocket, lollo rosso lettuce, lamb's lettuce and pak choi – and there are hundreds of varieties available as seeds. For variety, though, you could also buy a pack of mixed salad seeds.

Tomato leaves and stems are poisonous to young children, so they are best avoided if you are likely to have toddlers wandering around. Other plants that do well are courgettes, French beans, sweetcorn and peppers.

If you don't think you're green-fingered, and have never grown your own food before, don't be put off. Just imagine the thrill of tucking into a juicy corn on the cob with your grandchild, having picked it from your own garden!

Granny's House of Fun

Making the children's visit to your house fun is what being a twenty-first-century granny is all about. Long gone are the days when children visiting their grandparents were expected to be seen and not heard, speak when they were spoken to, and were forced to sit on the sofa listening to grown-up talk all day. How they must have dreaded such visits!

These days, one in two people aged fifty-four is a grandparent, so grannies are often younger and fitter than in years gone by. And with more mums returning to work, they are also much more likely to be playing a major role in general childcare.

With mum and dad often too busy to spend a great deal of time playing with the kids, the most important things you can give your grandchildren are time and attention. They are valuable commodities and the children are guaranteed to look forward to the next time Granny is in charge!

THINGS TO KEEP AT HOME

The amount of paraphernalia you keep at home for your grandchildren will, of course, be dictated by storage space, but here are a few suggestions.

Assorted jigsaw puzzles and board games

To save money, look out for games at jumble sales, fairs and in charity shops. Jigsaws can be bought very cheaply from the bargain stores.

Dressing-up box

Instead of throwing out old clothes, hats, shoes and bags, keep them all in a trunk or an old suitcase and have dressing-up days.

Paper, pens and paints

Stacks of old paper mean hours of fun with the kids, and if you've got a place where they can be messy with paints, that's even better, especially if mum's not keen on hosting painting sessions at home. A word of warning though – try not to send them home with their best outfit covered in paint!

'If becoming a grandmother was only a matter of choice, I should advise everyone straight away to become one.'

HANNAH WHITHALL SMITH

Collage materials

Old bits of ribbon, wrapping paper, silver foil wrappers and sequins are perfect for an arty afternoon. Also, building up collections of buttons, feathers, beads and scraps of material will prove useful in the long-term.

Outdoor games

Always keep a ball or two in the garage. A football is essential, even if you don't have a garden, as you can always take it to the park. If space is limited, an inflatable beach ball is a good idea. If you have plenty of storage, you might like to pick up some cheap cricket bats and tennis rackets.

Paddling pool

For hot days, nothing is more fun than splashing about in a paddling pool. But be extra careful if you have young grand-children, and *never* leave them unattended near the water.

THINGS TO DO
AT HOME

Make your own play dough

Shop-bought play dough is expensive and often dries up very quickly. Rather than splashing out on a tub or two, you and the children could spend a fun-filled day making the dough to play with later.

You will need:
2 cups plain flour
1 cup salt
4 tbsp cream of tartar
2 cups water
2 tbsp vegetable or sunflower oil
food colouring

1. Mix the flour with the salt and cream of tartar in a pan.

2. Add the oil, water and colouring, and stir until smooth.

3. Cook on the hob on a low heat for 4–5 minutes, stirring constantly. The dough should thicken into a mashed-potato consistency. Then set aside to cool.

As soon as you can handle the dough, you can get creative with it, but make sure you store it in an airtight container when you've finished playing so that it keeps for a few months.

Caution: although the dough is made from edible ingredients, it should not be eaten as its high salt content could harm a child.

Scavenger hunt

Whether it be in the garden or in the home, your grandchildren will love a scavenger hunt, and the organization requires minimum effort from you!

All you need to do is to write out a list of items to be found, depending on the environment in which the hunt will take place. In the home, for example, your list could include a pencil, an eggcup, a comb and an object with flowers on it. In the garden, you could request a fallen leaf, a ball, a stick etc. The list can be as long as you like.

Give the list to each child, along with a bag for collecting the objects, and send them out to look. The first person to come back to you with all the correct items is the winner.

Perhaps you could think up a small prize to give the successful grandchild.

Note: grandparents are officially entitled to help the younger ones to win!

Wool hunt

This activity works best the more children there are to play.

Take several different-coloured wools and cut enough short lengths from each ball for each child to have one. Then hide the strands of wool around the house in bundles of the same colour, and tell the children how many colours they have to find.

The first child to return to you with strands of every colour is the champion wool hunter!

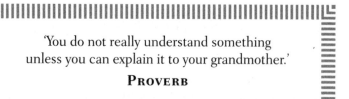

'You do not really understand something
unless you can explain it to your grandmother.'
PROVERB

Make-and-do kits

Most toy shops and supermarkets have an inexpensive range of craft kits that are great to stock up on. Girls can create their own jewellery or handbags, and boys can make dinosaurs, piggy banks and many other things.

If you want to buy these kits for a birthday or Christmas, or just an anytime gift, suggest keeping them at your house. You are much more likely to have the time to sit down with your grandkids and help them with the activities than their parents!

Dinosaur dig

This fun pastime is ideal if you have a sandpit or a rough area in the garden where you have ample room to pile up some sand.

Firstly, buy a dinosaur model kit with lots of parts (available at most toy and hobby stores). Number each separate part with a marker pen, so that you will know when each piece has been found, then bury the dino bones in a large quantity of play sand.

Give the children a new 2-inch paintbrush each, to give an authentic archaeological feel to the dig, and send them out to forage for the bones.

When the bones are all dug up, help the kids to build the dinosaur. A perfect way to spend an afternoon at Granny's!

Artful Advice

* Before you do anything, make sure you set up art projects in places where messy splodges are easy to clean up, and always put down a mat or old newspapers before you start.

* Keep an old jam jar as a water pot for painting, otherwise you might end up with paint stains all over your best china teacups!

* Even 'washable' paint doesn't always come out of clothes and many of the ready-mix paints stain *everything* . . . Keep a couple of old T-shirts to slip over the children's clothes to avoid getting in trouble with Mum and Dad.

* When your grandchild has put the finishing touches to his/her painting, if the subject of the masterpiece isn't immediately apparent, don't ask 'What is it?' Instead say, 'Tell me about your picture.'

* Keep a special place to exhibit their works of art. It doesn't have to be on your living room wall – a fridge, a kitchen notice board or a study wall are ideal.

* Buy a scrapbook. It's a really nice way of keeping the odd painting, card and letter for posterity.

* Don't try to keep everything your grandchild creates – you'll disappear under a mountain of paper in no time!

Potato printing

You may remember doing this with your own children or even when you were a child yourself, so why not repeat the experience with your grandchildren?

You will need:
several large potatoes
paper or cardboard
pencil
sharp knife
poster or ready-mix paint
paper plates

1 Cut your potatoes in half (make sure *you* do this bit, and not your grandkids, as you don't want any accidents).

2 Get your grandchild to draw a simple shape on a piece of paper. A star, a moon, a fish and a smiley face are all good things to start with.

3 Cut out the shape and trace it onto the cut surface of the potato.

4 Then, using the knife, carefully carve the background away, leaving the shape intact. (Again, *you* must do this tricky bit.)

5 Pour thin layers of the paint into ice-cream containers or paper plates.

6 Dip the carved potato into the paint and firmly press onto a piece of paper to create a clear impression of the shape.

7 When your grandkids have had enough of one shape, use the other half of the potato and start again.

7 If you don't want to use paint, you can colour the potato with felt-tip pens, but the effect is much fainter.

Whatever you do, don't throw the potato in the hotpot when you've finished!

Pasta picture

Kids love making these simple pictures and you can probably use the contents of your store cupboard so it's cheap too. Make sure you put a mat or newspaper on your table first, though. It can get messy!

You will need:
pasta of various shapes, sizes and colours, e.g. penne,
farfalle (bows), macaroni, fusilli, etc.
food colouring
newspaper
polythene bags
rice
margarine tubs
paper
craft or PVA glue

1 If your pasta is not coloured, place a handful of pasta shapes into a polythene bag, such as a freezer bag, and add a few drops of food colouring.

2 Shake well and then turn out onto newspaper to dry.

③ Repeat with as many different pastas and colours as you wish.

④ Place the rice into a few separate containers (such as empty margarine tubs) and mix a drop or two of food colouring into each. Add more drops if you want a stronger shade. Leave to dry.

⑤ Put all the dried pasta shapes and rice into different containers in the middle of the table or activity area (on newspaper, of course).

⑥ The children can either draw a picture and then glue on the pasta and rice, or create a freestyle 'mosaic' by sticking on the shapes randomly.

⑦ Allow the glue to dry before lifting the picture up – you wouldn't want to ruin this masterpiece!

Note: once the marvellous pictures are created, send them home with the kids. They do have a tendency to leave bits all over the house, even when dry, so Mum will have to deal with all that (just as you did in years gone by)!

Clarence the Caterpillar

This concertina character is great fun to make.

You will need:
1 piece of brightly coloured A4 paper
(preferably green or yellow)
ready-mix paints and a sponge
(or easy-paint bottles with sponge tops)
glue
stick-on eyes (optional)

pipe cleaners
thread or string
sticky tape
a straw

1 Fold your paper in half lengthways and cut along the crease. Sponge paint each side of the remaining half – a different colour each side – then leave to dry.

2 Fold the paper in half and in half again, lengthways.

3 Open out and cut along the creases, so that you have four strips.

4 Dab some glue on the end of one strip and glue another to it, at right angles.

5 Fold the lower strip over the top strip and crease it, then fold the other strip over the first and crease it. Continue folding alternate strips over each other to make a concertina shape.

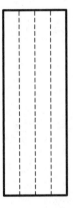

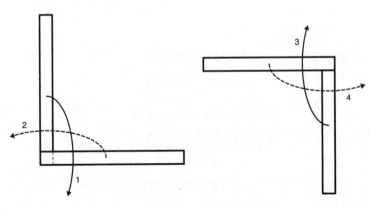

6 When you've almost finished folding the first two strips, glue the third and fourth strips on to each end of the folded strips, and continue the folding process as before.

7 When you've reached the end of the two strips, glue the two ends together to prevent the concertina from unravelling.

8 Next, choose which end will be the head, and stick on the eyes (or draw/paint them on).

9 Use the pipe cleaners to make feelers and legs.

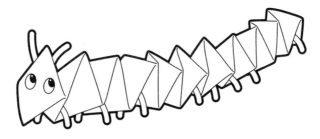

10 Fix a piece of thread behind the head and the tail using sticky tape, and attach the other ends to a straw so that you can make your caterpillar mobile by moving the straw up and down.

Note: you can also use this method to make a snake. Just leave the pipe cleaners out and add a tiny red forked tongue.

'Grandmother – a wonderful mother with lots of practice.'
AUTHOR UNKNOWN

Grannies in the Headlines

Being a gran doesn't mean sitting in a rocking chair and knitting all day, as these newsworthy third-agers have proved.

DANCING QUEEN

Supple octogenarian Marjorie Bradbury puts women less than half her age to shame. The eighty-nine-year-old great-granny can, literally, bend over backwards for her family. She can also do the splits, shoulder stands and put her legs behind her ears!

The former dance instructor from Manchester studied ballet and Greek dance from a young age, as well as playing hockey and tennis. 'It's no big deal,' she said modestly. 'I'm sure a lot of people can do it. I am not infallible.'

Although she gave up her dance classes in her seventies, the spirited lady still runs keep-fit classes for the over-fifties – she's her own best advert!

GRANNY RAP

Vivian Smallwood is a Californian grandmother who performs hip hop under the stage name Rappin' Granny (not to be confused with Rapping Granny, who was a regular on *The Howard Stern Show*). Born in 1933, Vivian began rapping to entertain her family after her son spotted her dancing across the room to a hip-hop beat.

After a few performances at home for her fourteen grandchildren and five great-grandchildren, Vivian released a little-known, self-titled music video in 1989. Seven years later she hit the headlines when she became a contestant on the hit television show *America's Got Talent* at the age of seventy-three. She made it through to the finals, but lost out to eleven-year-old singer Bianca Ryan.

In addition to her rapping talents, Vivian has also appeared in a few Hollywood films and TV series, including *Everybody Hates Chris*, *The Ladykillers* and *Malcolm in the Middle*.

* * *

CANNABIS GRAN

Grandmother Patricia Tabram became a poster girl for the pro-cannabis lobby when she was convicted of growing cannabis at her Northumberland home.

The sixty-eight-year-old was tried at Carlisle Crown Court after admitting that she used the drugs as an anti-depressant, and to relieve the constant pain she suffered after two car crashes. Conventional medicines, she claimed, had not worked and had left her feeling worse than before.

Growing the plants in a walk-in wardrobe, she regularly mixed cannabis powder into cakes, stir-fries and hot chocolate, and even wrote a cookbook, entitled *Grandma Eats Cannabis*. She also stood against Cabinet Minister Peter Hain in the 2005 general election as a representative of the Legalize Cannabis Alliance.

First convicted in 2005, she was given a suspended sentence, but two years later she was re-arrested and found guilty, and given a 250-hour community service order. Before her second trial, the defiant grandmother-of-two said she was not afraid of going to prison because she is 'everyone's granny' and would be 'treated like a queen'.

* * *

QUITE CONTRARY

Bored with aerobics classes, Bristol accountant Mary Athay decided to take up karate, and, in April 2007, by the age of sixty-two, she had earned a black belt. She can now break roof tiles and blocks of wood with her bare hands, but steers clear of breeze blocks in case she breaks a bone!

'It's very hard work, and getting a black belt was a huge achievement,' she said. 'My grandchildren think it's great fun to play-fight with me, but my husband never chats back to me now.'

She is now planning to take up sword training.

INSPIRATIONAL LADY

A horrific accident at the height of the troubles in Northern Ireland turned Emma Groves into a world-renowned campaigner.

In 1972, a rubber bullet from the gun of a British soldier hit her in the face as she stood in her West Belfast living room. As she woke up in her hospital bed, she was greeted by Mother Teresa of Calcutta, who told her the terrible news that she had lost both her eyes. Although Emma was distressed that she would never again see the faces of her eleven children or her grandchildren, this formidable lady was spurred into action by her tragic circumstances.

Together with her friend Clara Reilly, she helped to set up the United Campaign Against Plastic Bullets, which brought together bereaved families and highlighted the issues surrounding the use of rubber and plastic bullets.

She travelled the world, campaigning and talking to political leaders, addressed the European Parliament, and led a group of families to Scotland, where they stood outside a factory and informed the workers of the devastation caused by plastic bullets. She also lobbied shareholders of a production company in the USA, who immediately ended their involvement in the ammunition's manufacture.

When Emma died in 2007 at the age of eighty-six, she received a host of warm tributes from her huge family, which now included forty-two grandchildren and twenty-six great-grandchildren.

'She meant everything to everybody,' said granddaughter Sinead Groves. 'She was the head of the family, she kept us all together. She was a party animal and enjoyed a good get-together.

She was there for us all; children, grandchildren and great-grandchildren.

'She did not change after the shooting, she was still Granny. Her disability didn't disable her. Even for the younger great-grandchildren, she was just Granny.'

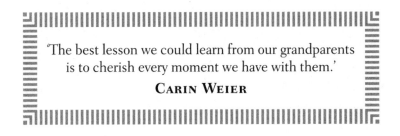

'The best lesson we could learn from our grandparents is to cherish every moment we have with them.'

CARIN WEIER

SENIOR SUPERSTAR

When Richard Grayson's grandmother was told she was dying, the writer decided to make her a star.

In 1980, after twenty years of ill health, eighty-year-old Sylvia Ginsberg of Miami was diagnosed with a brain aneurysm and told she had a maximum of one year to live. Sick of the shallow nature of celebrity culture, Richard decided it was time his grandma got her fifteen minutes of fame, so he set about making it happen.

First came a press release, announcing the launch of the Sylvia Ginsberg International Fan Club, along with a magazine, which included features such as 'Shocking: Why Sylvia Switched Supermarkets!', 'The Untold Story of Sylvia's Artificial Hips' and 'Sylvia's Love Quiz: Can You Pass It?'

Two days later the *Miami News* called and ran a story entitled 'Grandson Fans the Flames of Stardom for Sylvia.' Other journalists picked up the story and soon she was on front pages in Los Angeles, Minneapolis and Virginia.

As word spread, Sylvia was asked for autographs, reporters kept knocking on her door and neighbours started giving quotes to newspapers about what a wonderful woman she was.

Sylvia took it all in her stride, telling one newspaper that she never had a sense of humour, didn't know how to tell a joke, and wouldn't appear on *The Johnny Carson Show*. 'It's too late,' she said firmly. 'Who needs it? I go to bed early.'

After a brief taste of the limelight, Sylvia sadly passed away – exactly one year after her diagnosis.

* * *

HALF-BAKED DECISION

Jenny Brown was delighted when she came second in a cake-baking competition at a Cambridgeshire fête, until she discovered she was the only entrant.

The sixty-two-year-old grandmother entered her Victoria sponge in the village fête at Wimblington and was voted the runner-up, but she was shocked when a friend revealed the lack of competition. The judges, chosen by the Wimblington Sports Committee, knocked a few points off the sponge because of marks left by the oven rack.

'My friend came over to me at the fête and said I had come second,' explained Jenny. 'I asked her how many more entries there had been, but she just started laughing and said I was the only one.'

The sole entry took it well, however, and added, 'I definitely wasn't annoyed about it.'

RECORD-BREAKING GRANNY

Cathie Jung may be seventy, but she's no victim of middle-aged spread. In fact she's the proud owner of the smallest waist in the world.

Her tiny midriff measures just 15 inches and has landed her a place in the *Guinness World Records* book. The grandmother from North Carolina measures 39-15-39 and has been training her waist with corsets since she was forty-five. Her method has seen her shrink by 11 inches from her original 26-inch waist.

She first wore a corset when she was twenty-two, at her wedding to husband Bob, and later developed a fascination with Victorian clothing.

'I decided to start doing "tight lacing" and wearing a corset all the time,' she revealed. 'My three children were grown up, so I decided to go for it. It is the time of your life when you figure begins to head south and you start to feel frumpy, so I thought it would be a good way to feel elegant and sexy.'

Despite her astonishing figure, Cathie insists that she is perfectly healthy and has had X-rays to prove that the corsets have not harmed her. Luckily, her husband is an orthopaedic surgeon and has confirmed that the corsets actually support the spine rather than damage it.

'Everything in the midriff is flexible,' said Cathie.

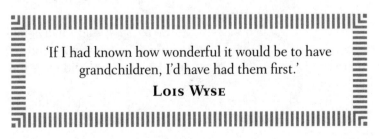

'If I had known how wonderful it would be to have grandchildren, I'd have had them first.'
LOIS WYSE

Days Out With Granny

Pedal power

With the recent resurgence in bike riding, many big parks, rural areas and cities have safe cycle paths for you and the children. Many will also have cycles for hire, if you don't own any yourself. These may also have attachments for putting babies and toddlers in while you pedal.

Make sure the smaller riders are competent on two wheels and always ensure that the whole family wear helmets. Details of cycle routes in your area are available on www.enjoyengland.com or from the Visit Britain office on 020 8846 9000. Information on the National Cycle Network can be found at www.sustrans.org.uk or by phoning 0845 113 0065. Alternatively, ask at your nearest tourist information office.

Shop till they drop

The idea of taking the kids shopping may sound dull, but you can easily make it into a fun day out. If they have a birthday coming up, get them to choose their own present (within reason, of course). You can even give them a budget. That way, not only will they get something that they really want, but they will also learn a little about how much those 'cheap' plastic toys really cost! Getting them to hand money over and count the change is also a good way of improving their maths skills.

As the children get older they will enjoy shopping trips with you more and more (especially the girls). Treat them to a lunch out and make it an occasion. Always be careful of pester power though – apparently it works better on grannies than on parents!

Film fun

Cinema tickets are surprisingly reasonable for children and the over-sixties, and the multiplexes usually have something for everybody's taste.

Find out what's playing at your local by calling them or looking on their website, and then give the children a choice of what to see. Try not to choose anything too long if the children are very young, and make sure the content and certificate of the film are suitable.

If you want to keep costs down, avoid the pick-and-mix sweets, popcorn and pop, as they are generally overpriced. Take your own snacks and drinks instead.

Tumble time

Soft play areas and play barns are worth mentioning as they weren't around when you were bringing up your children. They are huge hangar-like places that have soft climbing frames, slides, tunnels and ball ponds, adding up to loads of fun. Ask your local council or tourist information centre where your nearest one is.

Such venues really are a godsend on a rainy day and they usually aren't too expensive. But be warned: if you go in the school holidays, the noise created by hoardes of excited kids can be deafening!

Full steam ahead

Steam railways are still dotted about the country and are a great way to have a cheap day out. Many have themed days, such as Thomas the Tank engine events, but any journey will be fun for the children. Some have destinations at castles or adventure grounds and others just end up in villages and towns.

Choose where you want to go beforehand. It needn't cost a fortune as you could take a picnic and head for a nice park. For information on railways in your area, contact your local tourist information centre or go to www.heritagerailways.com, which has a useful map.

Fruity fun

Fruit-picking is a great day out for everyone, and there's no better way to encourage kids to eat healthy food than getting

'Grandmas never run out of hugs or cookies.'
Author Unknown

them to pick it themselves. Strawberries, raspberries and blackberries are the most common crop, but there are also farms that have apples, pears and even vegetables such as beans and broccoli. The hardest part is stopping the kids from eating all the fruits of their labour before they are paid for!

For your nearest PYO farm, check out www.pickyourown.org.uk, which is very helpful. It also has lots of tips on pickling and preserving the fruit.

To avoid disappointment it is a good idea to call the chosen farm before you go, as weather conditions and heavy picking can affect crops and hours of business.

Oh, and don't forget your wellies!

Teddy bears' picnic

A picnic in the park is always fun, but it can be even better for the little ones if you make it a themed event. For a teddy bears' picnic, get them to bring along one or two of their favourite bears each and make the food match the day. Sandwiches can be cut in the shape of bears, and bear crisps and biscuits are on sale in most supermarkets. You could include marmalade sandwiches (Paddington's favourite) or honey sandwiches (Isn't it funny how bears love honey!). Take a doll's tea set if you have one, or a small cup and saucer for bear, and involve the toys in the party.

Doll's tea parties are another alternative, particularly if your grandchild is more into dolls than bears, and you could take the idea a few steps further with a little imagination. How about a pirate picnic, with a treasure hunt thrown in? Or a fairy picnic? Get the kids to dress up for it and carry the theme throughout the day.

Be advised, though, that you can end up feeling a bit silly if you take it too far. It's never advisable for granny, whatever her age, to prance around the park in a fairy outfit!

Be the TV audience

Studio audiences are needed for a huge variety of shows and the tickets are absolutely free. Kids will be so excited at the thought of going to see their favourite show, that you will be the coolest granny around. The Internet is the best place to find them, but you can also make phone enquiries. Below are some of the websites and numbers available. Alternatively you can ring the TV companies' local offices.

BBC shows: **www.bbc.co.uk/showsandtours/tickets**

TV Recordings: **www.tvrecordings.com**

Lost in TV: **www.lostintv.com**
Telephone: 020 8530 8100

Beonscreen Ltd: **www.beonscreen.com** / **www.beonlive.com**
Telephone: 08700 632 932

Standing Room Only: **www.sroaudiences.com**
Telephone: 020 8684 3333

Clappers Ltd: **www.clappers-tickets.co.uk**
Telephone: 020 8532 2770/1

Applause Store: **www.applausestore.com**
Telephone: 020 8324 2700

'They say genes skip generations. Maybe that is why grandparents find their grandchildren so likeable.'
JOAN MCINTOSH

Silver-haired Stars of the Silver Screen

The Blue Bird (1940)
Starring Shirley Temple

THE PLOT
Mytyl (Shirley Temple) is the spoilt, selfish daughter of a woodcutter who finds a unique bird in the Royal Forest and refuses to give it to her sick friend. That night she and her brother are visited by a fairy named Berylune who sends them to search for the Blue Bird of Happiness. The children have a number of adventures including a visit with their (deceased) grandparents.

THE GRANDMA
Granny and Grandpa Tyl, played by Cecelia Loftus and Al Shean, are found in a place called the Land of the Past where they explain, in very sweet dialogue, that they are not dead but sleeping.

'Every time you think of us we wake up and see you again,' explains Granny Tyl.

'But we thought you were dead,' says Mytyl.

'No, dear,' replies Granny Tyl. 'Only when we're forgotten.'

GOOD GRANNY RATING
5/5 for being so sweet and touching

On Golden Pond (1981)
Starring Katharine Hepburn, Henry Fonda and Jane Fonda

THE PLOT
Elderly couple Ethel (Hepburn) and Norman (Fonda) Thayer are spending their summer at their house on Golden Pond when estranged daughter Chelsea (Jane Fonda) turns up with her boyfriend and his thirteen-year-old son Billy Ray. After dredging up old conflicts with her father, Chelsea leaves her parents to care for Billy Ray while she takes a trip to Europe.

THE GRANDMA
Katharine Hepburn won an Oscar for her delightful portrayal of Ethel, who provides family stability through thick and thin. She adores her husband, but is often stuck between him and their daughter. Billy Ray ends up being the catalyst that heals the rift.

GOOD GRANNY RATING
4/5 for being a wonderful granny and wife, although she's not so good at motherhood

Terms of Endearment (1983)
Starring Shirley MacLaine, Debra Winger and Jack Nicholson

THE PLOT
The film covers three decades in the lives of Aurora Greenaway (MacLaine), a fiercely protective mother, and her daughter Emma (Winger). Disapproving of her daughter's marriage, Aurora is horrified at the prospect of becoming a grandmother. Although she grows fond of her three grandchildren, in a grudging way, she hates her son-in-law and feels vindicated when he has an affair.

THE GRANDMA
Another Oscar-winning performance in a grandmother role, this time for Shirley MacLaine. The irascible, stubborn Aurora comes through for the children when she is needed.

GOOD GRANNY RATING
3/5 for being a fantastic character

Peggy Sue Got Married (1986)
Starring Kathleen Turner and Nicolas Cage

THE PLOT
Peggy Sue (Turner) is a forty-three-year-old mother who is about to divorce errant husband Charlie (Cage). At her high-school reunion she faints and is transported back to her teens. Faced with living her life over again, with hindsight will she make the same choices?

THE GRANDMA

Veteran Hollywood star Maureen O'Sullivan appears in a small role as Elizabeth Alvorg, the grandmother Peggy gets to revisit. A touching scene has Peggy answering the phone to her long dead grandmother and not knowing quite what to say.

GOOD GRANNY RATING

4/5 for playing a pivotal part in her granddaughter's life – even after her death

Grandma's House (AKA Grandmother's House) (1988)

Starring Ida Lee, Eric Foster and Kim Valentine

THE PLOT

The movie plays on a child's fear of aloof grannies and creepy old houses as two children, David and Lynne, are sent to live with their grandparents after the death of their father. When a dead body is found nearby, and neighbours suggest it's not the first, they begin to suspect their dear old granny and granddad are serial killers.

THE GRANDMA

If your grandchildren have lost both their parents and have come to live with you, it's best not to scare the living daylights out of them. Both Grandma and Grandad are creepy as can be in this atmospheric horror movie – and that can't be good for the poor orphaned kids!

GOOD GRANNY RATING

1/5 for taking the grandkids in to start with

The Princess Diaries (2001)
Starring Anne Hathaway and Julie Andrews

THE PLOT
The fifteen-year-old daughter of a single mum discovers that she is the princess of a small European principality. The death of her absent father, the crown prince of Genovia, means she is next in line to the throne. While she chooses between life as an American teenager and a role on the throne, she takes lessons in being a princess from her blue-blooded grandmother.

THE GRANDMA
Queen Clarisse Renaldi (Andrews) is well bred and elegant, but her initial interest in her socially inept granddaughter is fuelled by a desire to protect the Royal bloodline. While teaching Mia (Hathaway) how to become a princess, she also learns a thing or two about family and love.

GOOD GRANNY RATING
3/5 for final effort

'Grandchildren don't make a woman feel old;
it's being married to a grandfather that bothers her.'
AUTHOR UNKNOWN

Health Warning

One of the things to remember when your grandchildren come along is that you're not as young as you were when you had your own children. Taking charge of the little darlings is fraught with danger, so here are a few hazards to watch out for.

1 New technology in the baby carriage department hasn't made buggies, prams and pushchairs any easier to fold or unfold, so the likelihood of getting blistered and bleeding fingers is high. If in doubt, ask a friendly mum to help.

2 Car seat buckles are notorious pinchers, and, if your two-year-old grandchild decides to arch his back to prevent you doing it up, you're scuppered! When in doubt, try bribery, because physically pushing him or her into the seat with one hand while doing up the three-way buckle with the other is not only painful for both of you, it's virtually a physical impossibility.

3 Getting a hefty toddler in and out of the car seat is also a crunch moment – literally. Many a grandparent's back has been wrenched by this activity and it might take weeks to recover. Take it easy and be careful how you lift.

4 Young children are germ factories. The minute one child at school or nursery sneezes, they are all coming down with something and, in all probability, so are you. Colds, flu and stomach bugs are all part of being Granny. And the annoying thing is that while the kids might shake it off in a day, it may well wipe you out for weeks!

5 Remember Nitty Nora, the nurse who used to come round and inspect your hair at school? She was there for good reason! Nits do the rounds of schools and nurseries in frequent cycles and while you might think you're past the age of head lice, no one is immune. If you have had contact with a nit-infested grandchild, always check your own hair and comb through with conditioner and a nit comb.

6 Playtime can be exhausting with young children, and can also cause one or two minor injuries. Obviously sporting activities are good for all, but if you take to playing football or tennis in the garden, be careful of injury. Even more sedate play, such as jigsaws, might mean getting down on the floor. Just make sure that you can get up again!

'Always and Forever is a Grandmother's love.'
AUTHOR UNKNOWN

SOCIAL DANGERS

1. Becoming a bore is a common mistake made by proud grannies. Not all your friends will appreciate a weekly viewing of thirty new photographs of little Johnny!

2. It is also essential to remember that not everything your grandchild says or does is cute to other people. The occasional well-chosen funny story is great, but when you find yourself repeating every word your little darlings utter to a circle of fixed, polite smiles, change the subject!

3. Be careful in the playground. You may think the lady standing next to you is another granny, but she could just be an older mum. Think before you speak!

4. As desperate as you are to see your grandchildren whenever possible, you may let other hobbies and social engagements slip. Don't give up things you enjoy as you may well regret it when the family doesn't need you so much. You're not contractually obliged to say 'yes' *every* time you're asked to babysit, and your own social life is important too.

5. Your bank balance may well suffer. There is nothing a granny likes more than buying little gifts for their grandchildren, but don't be tempted to go mad if you can't afford it.

6. You stop being house-proud. After decades of keeping the home spotless and tidy, grannies are apt to find that they no longer care, as long as the kids are having fun. Before you know it, you'll have them drawing on the windows, splattering paint all over your best tablecloth and kicking footballs at the flowers – all the things your own children were never allowed to do!

Storytime With Grandma

One of the loveliest activities for a granny is reading the children a bedtime story. It's important that kids become familiar with books from an early age, and reading to them at night is a comforting, soothing routine that can calm them down before lights out.

You needn't spend a fortune on books either. Charity shops, jumble sales and nearly-new sales are great places to get bargain books, or you could join the local library and have an endless free supply.

There are thousands of titles to choose from, of course, but here are a few grandparent-related stories you might like to read.

AGES 2–5

Supersonic Tonic by Stephanie Rosenheim; illustrated by Elena Odriozola (Meadowside Books)
A sweet rhyme with beautiful illustrations, *Supersonic Tonic* is the story of a little girl who makes a potion to cure her ailing Granddad, with hilarious results.

Spot Visits His Grandparents by Eric Hill (Puffin)
A fun lift-the-flap book about Spot the Dog's stay at his grandparents' house, where he learns more about his Mum's younger days.

Grandma and Grandpa by Helen Oxenbury (Puffin)
Beautifully illustrated book about a small girl's wonderful week at her grandparents' house.

My Grandma is Wonderful by Nick Butterworth (Candlewick Press)

Nick Butterworth's excellent illustration and storytelling brings Grandma to life.

Vegetable Glue by Susan Chandler; illustrated by Elena Odriozola (Meadowside Books)
A funny and enchanting cautionary tale that is not only entertaining, but also teaches children the importance of eating vegetables.

AGES 6–10

George's Marvellous Medicine by Roald Dahl (Puffin)
Popular children's author Roald Dahl's portrayal of George's miserable grandmother is typically dark, but very funny.

Charlie and the Chocolate Factory by Roald Dahl (Puffin)
Unlike the grandma in *George's Marvellous Medicine*, the four dotty grandparents in this wonderful tale are sweet and engaging.

Astro Gran by Nick Ward (Meadowside Books)
A boy and his dear old Gran are blasted into space in his inventor dad's latest creation.

A Long Way From Chicago by Richard Peck (Puffin)
A little more advanced (eight and upwards), but a very amusing tale of a brother and sister's annual trip to see Grandma in her small town.

Alice's World Record by Tim Kennemore (Andersen Press)
Middle child Alice suffers from living with her tantrum-prone brother, Oliver, and a mischievous sister. On a visit to Grandma, who favours Oliver in everything, Alice is determined to make her brother reveal his true colours.

The World's Greatest Grannies

GRANNY SMITH

We've all eaten the apple, but how many people know who the real Granny Smith was?

In fact, the juicy green fruit is named after a British lady called Maria Ann Sherwood, born in Peasmarsh, East Sussex, in 1799. At nineteen, she married Thomas Smith and they lived in Kent until 1838, when they and several other families in the area were encouraged to emigrate to Australia where their agricultural knowledge was in much demand.

The Smiths sailed for New South Wales, accompanied by their five children, aged between sixteen and one, and Thomas found work with a wealthy Australian auctioneer at Kissing Point, Ryde, for £25 a year plus rations.

In the 1850s, Thomas bought 24 acres of land for £605, where they set up a fruit farm that included extensive orchards. Here, Maria experimented with her own seedlings and grew new varieties of fruit.

The first account of the origin of the Granny Smith

apple appeared in an article by local historian, Herbert Rumsey, in the *Farmer and Settler* magazine of 25 June 1924.

In it, fruit grower Edwin Small said that, in 1868, he and his father had been invited by Maria Smith to examine a seedling on her farm that had been developed from a crab apple.

Sadly, Maria Smith didn't live to enjoy the fruits of her labour (forgive the pun). She died in March 1870 before the variety became a commercial success.

GRANDMA MOSES

Grandma Moses became one of America's most celebrated artists after taking up painting in her seventies. The hardworking farmer's wife and mother of ten started life as Anna Mary Robertson in September 1860. As a child she drew on wood, using fruit juice as paint, and when her father bought sweets for her nine siblings, Anna would receive the drawing supplies she preferred.

She married Thomas Solomon Moses in 1887 and they settled on a farm in Eagle Bridge, New York. When a doctor told her to stop working in the farm because of her arthritis and neuritis, the grandmother of eleven turned to painting 'to keep busy and out of mischief'.

In 1938, when she was seventy-eight, Grandma Moses' pictures caught the eye of an art collector who saw them hanging in her local drugstore. A year later a hugely successful exhibition of her work was hosted in New York and word spread throughout the country. She was featured on radio, on television and in magazines and became an overnight sensation.

In an interview with *Time* magazine Anna, by then a great-grandmother of ten, said 'When I had my children and grandchildren, I was about as busy as they were. I never had much good of them. I have more time now for my great-grandchildren.'

Nonetheless, she continued to paint her hugely popular rural scenes and exhibit them throughout America, Europe and Japan. At the age of 100, she illustrated Clement Moore's now classic rhyming text *A Visit from St Nicholas* (otherwise known as *'Twas the Night Before Christmas*).

Grandma Moses outlived all her children, and, when she died at the age of 101, she was survived by her daughter-in-law Dorothy, nine grandchildren and a host of great-grandchildren numbering more than thirty.

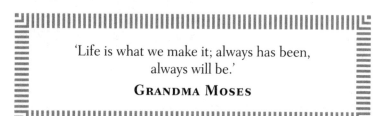

'Life is what we make it; always has been, always will be.'

GRANDMA MOSES

QUEEN VICTORIA

A formidable lady, Queen Victoria became known as the 'Grandmother of Europe' after many of her children and grandchildren married into the royal families of other European countries.

She ascended to the throne in 1837 at the age of eighteen. Three years later she married her first cousin, Prince Albert of Saxe-Coburg-Gotha, and in the following years she had nine children, all of whom survived to adulthood, which was rare at the time.

The death of her beloved husband in 1861 threw Queen Victoria into a period of deep mourning, which was to last ten years. Even after she retuned to public life, she always dressed in black, and, on her death in 1901, she was buried with a portrait of her Prince beside her.

An austere figure in her mourning dresses, although Queen Victoria may have seemed a frightening sight to small children, she was a warm and loving person who put great stock by family.

A grandmother at thirty-nine and a great-grandmother twenty years later, Queen Victoria was proud of her youthful looks and wrote to her daughter, 'I own it seems funny to me to be a grandmamma and so many people tell me they can't believe it!'

Although she wouldn't have seen much of her European family, she was an adoring granny and great-granny when she could spend time with them.

Christmas, a joyous occasion for Victoria until the death of her beloved Albert on 14 December, remained a family occasion even throughout her mourning. The Queen always spent the day at Osborne House on the Isle of Wight, surrounded by children, grandchildren and, latterly, great-grandchildren.

On the birth of grandson George, later King George V, she asked that he be called Frederick, but gave in to his parents preference. 'If the dear child grows up good and wise,' she wrote, 'I shall not mind what his name is.'

QUEEN ELIZABETH, THE QUEEN MOTHER

Children can often feel closer to their grandparents than their own parents and the Queen Mother was certainly a huge influence on Prince Charles throughout his life.

As her first grandchild, Charles was very precious to her, and when his mother, Queen Elizabeth II, was too busy with official duties, he turned to his grandmother for solace and guidance.

The Queen and the Duke of Edinburgh were often away on state visits abroad, and it was during these absences that Charles and his sister Anne grew close to the Queen Mother. When he went to boarding school at Gordonstoun, it was she to whom he turned to voice his unhappiness.

They shared a similar sense of humour and a special understanding. Royal biographer Anthony Holden said, 'More than either of Charles's parents, perhaps, his grandmother understood the ordeal of the quiet, uncertain child in a harsh and alien world.'

Born Elizabeth Bowes-Lyon in August 1900, she married Albert, Duke of York, in 1923 and had two children, Elizabeth and Margaret. Her world was turned upside down in 1936 when King Edward VIII abruptly abdicated to marry his mistress, Wallace Simpson, and Elizabeth's husband, who was next in line to the throne, became king.

It was a task that she believed detrimental to 'Bertie's' health and she never forgave her brother-in-law for thrusting it upon him. But if Bertie, now known as King George VI, suffered, the Queen's own indomitable spirit shone through.

In the Second World War, she gained the love of the nation by refusing to leave London and by visiting bombed-out communities to offer moral support. Her actions raised morale so much that Adolf Hitler called her 'the most dangerous woman in Europe.'

Widowed in 1952, she became the family matriarch on the death of Queen Mary a year later, and remained the most beloved member of the Royal family until her death in 2002.

The Prince of Wales called her 'one of the most remarkable and wonderful people in the world' and shortly after her death he said he missed her 'more than I can possibly say'.

As well as being a real grandmother to six, Queen Elizabeth, the Queen Mother held such a place in the hearts of the British people that she became known as 'grandmother of the nation.'

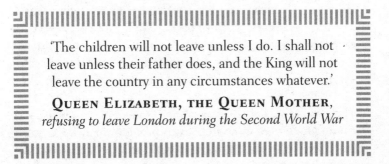

'The children will not leave unless I do. I shall not leave unless their father does, and the King will not leave the country in any circumstances whatever.'

QUEEN ELIZABETH, THE QUEEN MOTHER,
refusing to leave London during the Second World War

BARONESS (MARGARET) THATCHER

When Margaret Thatcher's first grandchild Michael was born, Britain's first and only female Prime Minister famously announced her new status with the line 'We have become a grandmother.'

Using the 'Royal we', previously reserved for the monarch, led to much ridicule and some suggestions that power had gone to her head, but the moment also showed that even one as

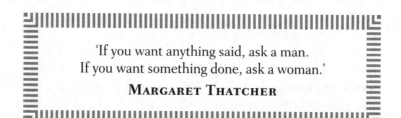

> 'If you want anything said, ask a man.
> If you want something done, ask a woman.'
> **MARGARET THATCHER**

tough as the Iron Lady could be touched by the unique moment of becoming a grandma for the first time.

Born Margaret Hilda Roberts in 1925, the daughter of a Grantham grocer, she married Denis Thatcher in 1951 and qualified as a barrister in 1953, the same year her twins, Carol and Mark, were born. After becoming MP for Finchley six years later, she rose through the ranks of the Conservative party to become leader in 1975. A landslide election in 1979 was the start of an eleven-year term as Prime Minister, the longest ever served in the UK.

The core values at the root of her Conservative ideals, she attributed to her grandmother. 'I was brought up by a Victorian grandmother,' she said. 'We were taught to work jolly hard. We were taught to prove yourself; we were taught self-reliance; we were taught to live within our income.

'You were taught that cleanliness is next to Godliness. You were taught self respect. You were taught always to give a hand to your neighbour. You were taught tremendous pride in your country. All of these things are Victorian values. They are also perennial values. You don't hear so much about these things these days, but they were good values and they led to tremendous improvements in the standard of living.'

Teenagers Revisited

There will come a time when your gorgeous, cute and clever grandchild turns into a grumpy, hormone-filled monster. You may well remember a similar thing happening to your own sweet children!

If you're lucky, all the sarcasm and anger will be directed at their parents and you'll get off scot-free. But don't be surprised if you are no longer their favourite person and they are more interested in going to see their pals than visiting Grandma.

'When grandparents enter the door,
discipline flies out the window.'

Ogden Nash

HOW TO GET THROUGH TO YOUR TEENAGE GRANDCHILDREN

DO:

Take up a computer course

New technology is not reserved solely for the young. Silver surfers are all the rage and there's no better way to surprise your teenage grandchildren than by knowing more about computers than they do.

Take an interest in their interests

Whether it's drama, sport or reading books, find out about the subject and bring it up. If they support a football or rugby team, find out the names of the players and keep track of how they are doing. Sport may bore you rigid, but rest assured you'll get your reward in heaven!

Treat them as grown-ups

One of the biggest frustrations of being a teenager is that you don't feel like a child, but nobody treats you as an adult. Suggest doing grown-up pursuits like board and card games, and take them to restaurants and cafes rather than a burger bar.

Start each conversation with an open question

If a question requires a 'yes' or 'no' answer, chances are that's what you'll get – with attitude. Instead, try asking questions that require a sentence reply, such as 'What have you been doing today?' or 'What have you got planned for the weekend?'

Keep up with showbiz gossip

Surf the net or buy the odd celebrity magazine. That way you might occasionally know what on earth they are talking about!

DON'T:

Start every sentence with 'when I was a girl'

Reliving the good old days may be one of the joys of getting older, but teenagers are easily bored. Keep your nostalgia to yourself, except for a few select stories which will truly amaze.

Buy (or download) the same music as them

It's one thing to know who they are talking about, but quite another to be rushing out to buy the latest rap album to impress them. They won't be impressed, they'll be embarrassed!

Embarrass them in public

They may be your best friend when they are alone with you, but when they are with their own pals, keep your distance. If you see them in the street, say hello, but don't make a big fuss, and *never* baby them.

Play the tough parent

They get enough of that at home! If teenage moodiness is causing problems with their parents, your company should be a safe haven from the rows.

Take sides

If your teenaged grandchild has had a bust-up with mum, don't add to his or her anguish by saying 'Your Mum's right!' Nor should you side with your grandchild. Stay out of it.

THINGS YOU SHOULD NEVER SAY TO A TEENAGER

When I was your age I was out at work.

Ooh, your skin looks terrible today.

There are plenty more fish in the sea.

As your mum's away you can come home any time you like.

That's a lovely mini-skirt. Can I borrow it?

Of course you can borrow my mobile phone.

The youth of today have no manners.

You look really sweet in that outfit.

You Know You're a Granny When...

* You start saying 'Bless him' all the time.

* You find the slightest excuse to call your children.

* You walk past the designer dresses and head for the children's department at your favourite clothes store.

* Your children suddenly want to see a lot more of you.

* The most exciting event on your calendar is a toddler's birthday party.

* You can't pass a toy shop without buying a treat.

* You get competitive about a baby's ability to walk or talk.

* You actually look forward to changing nappies.

* You are immune to crying, whinging and tantrums and see only sweetness.

* Your house resembles a bombsite for the first time in years, and you don't care!

'A grandmother is a person with too much wisdom to let that stop her from making a fool of herself over her grandchildren.'
PHIL MOSS

Long-distance Granny

Grannies are not always on the doorstep, and it can be heart-breaking to be too far from your grandchild to see them on a regular basis. But that doesn't mean you can't be a big part of their lives.

Here are a few tips for long-distance grannies.

Use snail mail

In the days of telephones, text messages and e-mails, children rarely receive real letters. As a consequence they love to get something through the post, whether it is a letter, a postcard or a small package. Don't compensate for your absence by sending

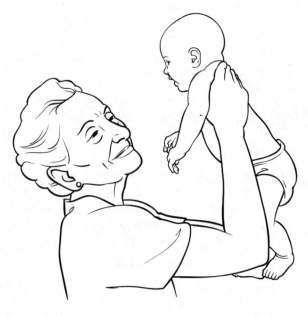

expensive gifts – a simple letter or a card telling them your news will be just as exciting for them.

Send photos

Your children will undoubtedly send you regular snapshots of their little darlings so that you can keep up to date, but it should be a two-way street. Granted your looks won't change on a regular basis, but if you go somewhere exciting and a photo is taken, send one to your grandchildren with a little note about the event.

Plan visits well

For your sake, and those of the child's parents, make sure you plan your trips well in advance. Always discuss with them when you will come and when you will be leaving, so they are in no doubt. If it is a long stay, plan days out with the children and give their parents some space.

Tell the children what you have planned

Send a letter, phone or e-mail and tell the kids what fun days lie ahead. They will love looking forward to your visit. But be careful – never promise a child something that you can't deliver.

> 'An hour with your grandchildren can make you feel young again. Anything longer than that, and you start to age quickly.'
> **GENE PERRET**

If something is weather dependent, for example, don't make any pledges until you know what the day will be like. ·

Offer to babysit

If you are staying more than a night or two, suggest that your son or daughter and partner take the opportunity to go out alone. If it is a long visit, and they feel they must spend every evening entertaining you, it may make life stressful. An evening out for them will break up the visit and give you time alone with the grandchildren.

Help out – to a point

Some mothers complain that their mother-in-law never lifts a finger, while others moan that she does too much and interferes in housework routines and cooking. Try to strike a happy medium. Offer to prepare dinner, lay the table or wash up, but don't be too pushy. You may be just as useful if you are keeping the kids occupied while mum or dad get on with routine domestic activities.

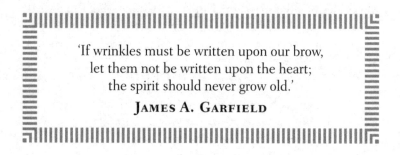

'If wrinkles must be written upon our brow,
let them not be written upon the heart;
the spirit should never grow old.'
JAMES A. GARFIELD

The Other Woman

If your grandchildren are lucky enough to have two grandmothers, you will need to handle your rival carefully. Whatever your previous relationship with your child's mother-in-law, jealousy is about to rear its ugly head in a way you wouldn't think possible.

After all, your children only had one mum, so there was no real rival for their affection. Now you have fallen in love all over again, and every moment your beloved grandchild spends with

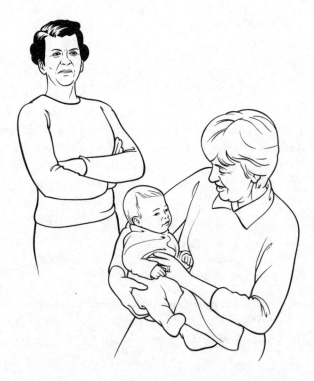

the other granny will make you feel like a jealous teenager whose first crush is eyeing up another girl!

Here are a few tips on handling the situation with as much dignity as possible.

* Whatever your relationship with the other granny before your grandchild was born, don't let that change. If you were great friends beforehand and spent time together, carry on, but don't bring baby along too. That will only complicate matters.

* If you rarely mixed before, don't let your children bludgeon you into big get-togethers unless you are comfortable sharing your family with the in-laws at such an event.

* If you do attend a social gathering together, be careful not to hog the grandchildren, as this will cause resentment.

* If your grandchildren are determined to spend all their time with you – you are the fun granny, after all – do the right thing. Discreetly suggest that they go and talk to Granny Number Two or steer them in her direction if they want help with a picture or a game.

* Conversation at such events should not revolve around the kids. You may like to swap stories, but don't let it turn into a competition. If it is heading that way, talk about something else.

* Never gloat! If you have a bigger garden, can afford more expensive gifts or have more time for days out, there's no need to rub it in.

✳ Inevitably, the other granny will have different ideas and ways of doing things. She may be more of a disciplinarian, or you may feel she spoils the children. Either way, she loves them as much as you do. *Never* criticize her in front of the kids.

✳ If your child or his/her partner moan about the other granny, don't be tempted to join in. Remember that harsh words could come back to bite you. Whatever the other granny has done to upset your brood, it is not your argument, so stay out of it.

✳ Accept her talents. The other granny may be a better cook, excellent at making things or fantastic at music. Don't compete in the same field, but find things you are good at and make it fun for the kids.

✳ Babysitting time should never become a competition. If geography, family closeness or just busy lives mean that you get to see less of the little ones than other grandparents, accept it. It might hurt, but you should make the most of the time spent with them rather than worrying about the time that someone else is spending with them.

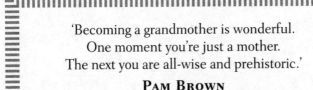

'Becoming a grandmother is wonderful.
One moment you're just a mother.
The next you are all-wise and prehistoric.'
PAM BROWN

* Research has shown that a child's maternal grandmother is likely to be the closest to the family, as daughters often turn to their mothers for help and advice, and tend to be closer to their mums than sons. This means that, if you are the paternal grandma, you may have to take a back seat and accept that your co-granny has more influence on the children's upbringing.

* If you feel you are not seeing enough of the children, don't start a fight or compare yourself to the other granny. Suggest your son or daughter might like a day off or a night out and ask to babysit. Few busy parents would turn that offer down!

THE IMPERFECT PARENTS

Remember that the arrival of a baby, particularly the first one, can put a strain on the best of relationships. Your son or daughter and their partner have a lot of adjusting to do and your behaviour could be a help or a hindrance.

Whatever you thought of your son-in-law or daughter-in-law before, they are now the parent of your grandchild and need your support and encouragement – not a sniping, overbearing mother-in-law.

Here are a few things to bear in mind.

* If you are the maternal grandmother and spend a lot of time with your daughter and the children, make sure you don't make dad feel left out. He may feel that you two are ganging up on him, which won't help your daughter's relationship at all.

* Dads today are very different than they were thirty years ago. He is as likely to be changing the nappies and getting up in the night as mum is, so don't assume he knows nothing about childrearing.

* If it is your son's baby who is the latest addition to the family, tread carefully. Remember how you were with your babies. A new mother has the instinct of a lioness, and can be just as fierce if crossed. She may take endless advice from her own mother, but that doesn't mean she'll appreciate yours!

* Never criticize your son or daughter's partner. Just as they will defend you, if you are being maligned, they will defend their partner rather than admit any faults.

* Stay out of their arguments. Your daughter may be on the phone in tears, telling you how mean hubby is, but you must never takes sides. Chances are the next day they'll be back in each others arms and negative comments from you could come back to haunt you.

* Always take the parents' line on important issues such as religion, manners and moral behaviour. You may not like the fact that your grandchild is being brought up with different values, but that is his/her parents' choice.

* Do praise the parenting skills of your child and his/her partner. No parent is ever sure they are doing everything right and grandparents are all too quick to criticize. How many people say 'You're a wonderful mum' or 'You're a great dad'? It can mean the world to a harassed parent.

* Praise the children to their parents, too. No mum or dad ever tires of hearing how clever, talented, kind or polite their child is.

* Don't compare one set of grandchildren to their cousins. Much as your offspring may love her nieces and nephews, she doesn't want to keep hearing how wonderful they are.

* Avoid a showdown. If things are building up to the stage where you may say something you'll regret, take a deep breath and step back.

* Learn how to say sorry. If an issue does come to the fore and harsh words are exchanged, there is no joy in standing your ground if it means losing your children and grandchildren. Pride will be no comfort then.

'When a child is born, so is a grandma!'
AUTHOR UNKNOWN

Granny's Words of Wisdom

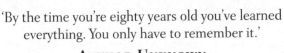

'By the time you're eighty years old you've learned
everything. You only have to remember it.'

AUTHOR UNKNOWN

Grandmothers have always been prone to producing an old
wives' tale for every occasion. But is she talking nonsense or
revealing pearls of wisdom that make perfect sense?

Ne'er cast a clout till May is out

The traditional phrase is often assumed to mean that you
shouldn't shed your winter clothes (clout) before the month of
May is over. However, many experts believe that 'till May is out'
actually refers to the blossom on the hawthorn bush, which is
known as May blossom. This bush, also known as the May tree,
is common in the English countryside, and flowers at the end of
April or early May. As the timing of blossom depends on the
warmth of the weather, it turns out to be sound advice indeed.

Toast always lands butter side down

This is true in over 90 per cent of cases and the reason is not
just Sod's Law, as you might imagine. It is largely down to the
height of the average kitchen counter, from which most of the
offending slices are dropped. The toast, which usually falls at
an angle, rotates as it descends because of its uneven weight,

which is caused by the spread butter. Because of the height it drops from, it only rotates halfway before hitting the floor. If dropped from twice the height it would, in most cases, rotate the full 360° and land butter side up.

Chocolate gives you spots

This assertion, long spouted by parents and grandparents to troubled teenagers with devastating acne, is a myth. Acne is caused by overproduction of oil that causes a partial blockage of a pore. Because this is influenced by hormones, it is more prevalent in teenagers. Many studies have examined the relationship between diet and acne, and none has ever found any conclusive evidence to support a link between chocolate or fried foods and spots.

Cheese gives you nightmares

Granny comes unstuck on this one. Recent research has shown that vitamin B6, found in large quantities in cheese, actually helps you to sleep. Studies of insomnia sufferers found they were often lacking in serotonin. In order to make more, the body requires vitamin B6, which is found in cheese, carrots, fish, lentils, peas, potatoes, sunflower seeds and wholemeal flour. So if you have sleepless nights, up your intake of these foods, and ignore granny's nightmare warning.

Cats always land on their feet

A cat's ability to fall from a great height and walk away unscathed has fuelled the myth that the animal has nine lives. Research conducted by two New York vets in 1987, who studied animals brought to them after falls of between two and thirty-two storeys, discovered that the most injuries were caused around seven storeys. Above that, bizarrely, the injury level decreased. The reason the cats fared so well in general was because of a high surface area to mass ratio, which means a lower velocity is reached. They are also more flexible and can twist mid-flight to land on their feet, absorbing the shock through the soft tissue of their legs. The 'seventh storey' is thought to be the height that enables them to reach their terminal velocity before hitting the ground. As they accelerate, they stiffen up with fright. After terminal velocity is reached, they are no longer accelerating and appear to relax, which explains why cats falling from higher storeys sustained fewer injuries.

N.B. It is not advisable to test this theory by throwing your pet out of the window of a high-rise building.

'God couldn't be everywhere,
so he created grandmothers.'
AUTHOR UNKNOWN

Black makes you look slimmer

This is the real reason that black never goes out of fashion. Black clothing works because we perceive shapes by the shadow and shades we see. These are not visible on black and, therefore, the shape appears more flat. It's great way to hide those lumps and bumps.

A silver spoon in the neck of an open champagne bottle retains the fizz

Some believe it is a stainless steel spoon but, in fact, this appears to be a myth. Winemaker Frédéric Panaïotis, from Veuve Clicquot, has revealed the results of an experiment conducted by the company that tested 180 open bottles of champagne. Some had a silver spoon inserted in the neck, some stainless steel spoons and some had none at all. The next day there was some fizz in all the bottles, but the spoon made no difference at all. Frédéric added, 'In all the bottles there was some oxidization, which you want to avoid. The best thing is to drink it all at once.' Sound advice.

Red sky at night, shepherds delight; Red sky in the morning, shepherds warning.

This old wives' tale does have some foundation of truth, but only in some parts of the world, including the UK. Clouds often appear red in the morning and evening because of the way the spectrum of colours breaks up as it passes through the atmosphere. At sunrise and sunset the light has further to travel than at other times, and red is able to travel further than the other colours without being diverted and is then reflected off the clouds. As the wind is mostly westerly in the UK, and the sun rises in the east and sets in the west, red sky at night means the clouds are in the east, and therefore are being blown away. A red sky in the morning means the clouds are in the west, and heading towards you. So now you know!

You can't get one cold straight after another

You certainly can. Actually, unless you look after yourself very well during a brief illness, you are more likely to catch another cold. The increased resistance you gain from being ill only works on exactly the same strain of virus, and the common cold comes in over 200 varieties.

Only eat shellfish when there is an 'r' in the month

When people used to gather their own shellfish, this was sound advice as toxic algae that affected the shellfish could multiply in these months. Also, in most European countries, oysters and other shellfish spawn in the months between May and August, when there is no 'r', so they are not marketed. In many other countries, including the US, they are now safe to eat all year round due to harvesting methods and improved hygiene regulations.

'What children need most are the essentials
that grandparents provide in abundance.
They give unconditional love, kindness, patience,
humour, comfort, lessons in life.
And, most importantly, cookies.'
RUDOLPH GIULIANI

Laughter is the best medicine

Granny is right on this one. Studies show that laughter boosts levels of endorphins, the body's natural painkillers, and decreases levels of epinephrine, the stress hormone.

A study at the University of Maryland Medical Centre in Baltimore also concluded that a good chuckle on a regular basis can lower the risk of a heart attack by 40 per cent. So a laugh a day may well keep the doctor away.

Don't try to teach your Grandma to suck eggs

The origin of this phrase is unknown, but the message is clear enough. Children should never presume to tell someone as experienced as their granny how to do something she has been doing all her life. Although why she'd be sucking eggs is something of a mystery!

Household Tips

Years of experience around the house means that daughters and sons may often ask you for advice. But if your idea of household hints is no more complicated than picking up the latest cleaning product from the local supermarket, your granny credentials need a boost. Here are a few traditional tips to pass on.

Lemon juice stops a cut apple from browning

When an apple is cut, its cells leak a product called phenolics, which mixes with the apple's enzymes and is then oxidized by contact with the air, turning the apple brown. Lemon juice contains the antioxidant vitamin C, which is clear when oxidized and prevents the phenolics from causing any browning.

Soda crystals are perfect for cleaning a washing machine

In the eco-friendly society we live in today, many people routinely wash at 30°C or 40°C. As a result, soap (particularly the non-biological brands) is not properly broken up. After a while the build-up can cause nasty smells and a maintenance wash is required. Pour a good dose (half a bag) of soda crystals into your empty drum and set the dial to a 90°C wash.

'A family with an old person
has a living treasure of gold.'
CHINESE PROVERB

Wash paintwork and walls with soda crystals

Expensive cleaning products can be harsh on paintwork, and soda crystals are not only cheaper but also more effective. Dissolve half a cup (75g or ½oz) for each pint of warm water and use a cloth to wipe over any surface.

Add a drop of vinegar to pans

When boiling puddings or eggs, add a little vinegar to avoid leaving any white watermarks.

Remove limescale marks with vinegar

If your bath or sink has a build-up of limescale, soak some cloths and rags in white vinegar, cover the mark and leave to soak overnight.

Add water to a grill pan

Before grilling greasy food, half fill the grill pan with water. When you have finished with the grill, tip the remaining water down the sink and wipe with a damp cloth and a little washing-up liquid.

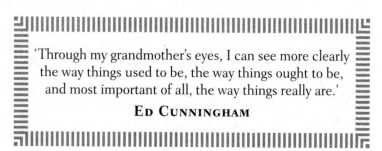

'Through my grandmother's eyes, I can see more clearly the way things used to be, the way things ought to be, and most important of all, the way things really are.'

ED CUNNINGHAM

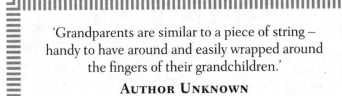

Cleaning up broken egg

If you drop an egg on the floor, pour salt over it and leave it for a few minutes. The egg will harden and be much easier to clean up.

Cleaning grease from a carpet

Pour baking soda over grease spots and brush through the pile of the rug. Leave overnight, then vacuum out.

Preventing pollen stains

If you are lucky enough to be given a bouquet with flowers prone to dropping pollen, such as lilies, take a piece of damp kitchen towel and gently wipe the pollen from each stamen.

Removing chewing gum

Discarded chewing gum has become an increasing problem in recent years, and in fabric and carpets, where it has been trodden in on the bottom of a shoe, it's difficult to shift. Freeze the gum with an ice cube to harden it before scraping it off, then gently wash the fabric or carpet.

A Song For Granny

From the memorable number-one hit 'There's No One Quite Like Grandma' to the quirky Christmas tune 'Grandma Got Run Over By a Reindeer', grannies of all kinds have been immortalized in a number of eclectic songs:

✳ 'Granny's Song' – SHEILA KAY ADAMS

✳ 'There's No One Quite Like Grandma' – ST WINIFRED'S SCHOOL CHOIR

✳ 'Grandma's Hands' – BILL WITHERS

✳ 'Grandmother's Song' – STEVE MARTIN

✳ 'Grandma' – MIKE JONES

✳ 'Grandma Told Grandpa' – LIGHTNIN' HOPKINS

✳ 'Hey Grandma' – ELECTRIC LIGHT ORCHESTRA

✳ 'Grandma's Feather Bed' – JOHN DENVER

✳ 'Grandma Got Run Over By a Reindeer' – ELMO and PATSY

✳ 'Granny' – DAVE MATTHEWS BAND

✳ 'Grandma's Party' – PAUL NICHOLAS

✳ 'A Song For Grandma and Grandpa' – JOHNNY PRILL

It's Never Too Late To ...

Join a pop group

In May 2007, a group of forty British pensioners came together to become singing sensation The Zimmers, a pop band with a combined age of over 3,000 years.

Their first single was a cover of The Who's 'My Generation', which they recorded at the famous Abbey Road studios in London. The video of the recording, posted on YouTube, received 1.5 million hits in a fortnight, and the song itself reached number 26 in the UK charts.

Three members of the group also embarked on a publicity tour to Los Angeles in the US, and appeared on *The Tonight Show With Jay Leno,* alongside movie star George Clooney.

* * *

Set up a blog

María Amelia López is a Spanish granny who calls herself 'the world's oldest blogger.' Ever since her grandson, Daniel, set up her Internet blog in December 2006 – a present for her ninety-fifth birthday – she has been regularly updating it.

Nicknamed 'the little granny' by her readers, she dictates her entries to Daniel, and uses her blog to describe aspects of her life to date, as well as offering her many insightful thoughts on modern life. 'It's like having a conversation,' she has said, 'and those who read what I say become my friends.'

At the time of writing, Mrs López's blog has received almost 850,000 hits.

The Joke's on Grandma

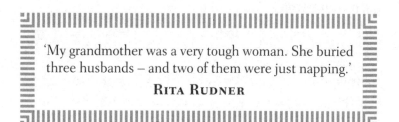

After playing outside with some friends, little Johnny came indoors to ask his granny a puzzling question.

'Granny,' he said. 'What is it called when two people are sleeping in the same room and one is on top of the other?'

A little shocked, his granny replied, 'It's called sexual intercourse.'

Satisfied with her answer, Johnny went back to playing with his friends. Minutes later, he stormed back into the house with a tear-stained face.

'Granny,' he said crossly. 'It is not called sexual intercourse! It's called bunk beds and Jimmy's mum wants to talk to you!'

* * *

A young boy and his doting grandmother were walking on the beach when a huge wave appeared out of nowhere, sweeping the child out to sea. The horrified woman fell to her knees, and started praying.

'Lord, return my grandson to me and I will be eternally grateful,' she wailed.

As she prayed, another huge wave built up and deposited the terrified child on the sand, at which Grandma stared angrily toward the heavens and remarked, 'When we came, my grandson had a hat!'

* * *

A hospital receptionist picked up the phone to a sweet old granny.

'Could I find some information on a patient, please,' she asked.

'Yes, of course,' replied the receptionist. 'What's the name and room number.'

'Lucy Mayes, room twenty-two,' said the old lady.

'I'll just check her notes,' the girl replied. 'Oh, good news. She's doing very well, making a speedy recovery and the doctor says she can go home on Wednesday. Are you a relative?'

'No,' answered the granny. 'I'm Lucy Mayes in room twenty-two. Nobody tells me anything!'

'My grandmother started walking five miles a day
when she was sixty. She's ninety-seven now
and we don't know where the hell she is.'
ELLEN DEGENERES

*The following account has been reported as a true story from the
US, but may well be an urban myth . . .*

Returning from a shopping trip, an elderly lady found four men
about to drive off in her car. She dropped her shopping bags and
pulled out a gun, then screamed at the top of her voice, 'I have a
gun and I know how to use it – get out of the car, you scumbags!'

The men jumped out of the car and ran for their lives, while
the old woman loaded her bags and got into the driver's seat.

Still shaken by the incident, she had trouble getting the key
into the ignition and, after a few tries, she suddenly realized
why. A few minutes later she found her own car parked four or
five spaces further down!

Horrified at her terrible mistake, she drove to the police
station and confessed all. The desk sergeant fell about laughing
and pointed to the other end of the counter. There stood four
pale, shaken men who were reporting a car-jacking by a mad
elderly woman described as white, less than 5 feet tall, with
curly, white hair, wearing glasses and carrying a large handgun.

No charges were filed.

*   *   *

One day, a ninety-five-year-old widow decided she was ready to join her late husband in heaven.

After finding his old army pistol, she decided the quickest way would be to shoot herself through the heart. Determined to make sure she got it right first time, she rang her doctor and asked exactly where she would find her heart.

'It's just below your left breast,' the helpful man informed her.

Later that night, she was admitted to the hospital with a gunshot wound to her knee . . .

* * *

When little Michael's grandma came to visit, he ran up and gave her a big hug.

'I'm so happy to see you, Granny,' he said excitedly. 'Now Daddy will have to do that trick he's been promising to do!'

'What trick is that, darling?' asked his grandmother, intrigued.

'I heard Daddy tell Mummy that he would climb the blooming walls if you came to stay with us again!'

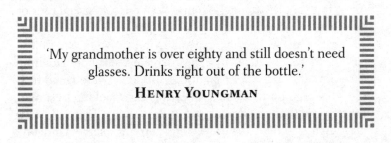

'My grandmother is over eighty and still doesn't need glasses. Drinks right out of the bottle.'

HENRY YOUNGMAN

Also available in this bestselling series:

The Boys' Book: How To Be The Best At Everything
ISBN: 978-1-905158-64-5   Price: £7.99

The Girls' Book: How To Be The Best At Everything
ISBN: 978-1-905158-79-9   Price: £7.99

The Mums' Book: For The Mum Who's Best At Everything
ISBN: 978-1-84317-246-8   Price: £9.99

The Dads' Book: For The Dad Who's Best At Everything
ISBN: 978-1-84317-250-5   Price: £9.99

The Family Book: Amazing Things To Do Together
ISBN: 978-1-906082-10-9   Price £14.99

The Christmas Book: How To Have The Best Christmas Ever
ISBN: 978-1-84317-282-6   Price: £9.99

And coming soon:

*The Grandads' Book: For The Grandad
Who's Best At Everything*
ISBN: 978-1-84317-308-3   Price: £9.99

These titles and all other Michael O'Mara Books
are available by post from:
Bookpost Ltd
PO Box 29
Douglas
Isle of Man
IM99 1BQ

To pay by credit card, use the following contact details:
Telephone: 01624 677237 / Fax: 01624 670923
Email: bookshop@enterprise.net
Internet: www.bookpost.co.uk

Postage and packing is free in the UK;
overseas customers should allow £5 per hardback book.